Getting Around After 60

A PROFILE OF BRITAIN'S OLDER POPULATION

by Claire Jarvis, Ruth Hancock
Janet Askham, Anthea Tinker

A report by the Gerontology Data Service
at the Age Concern Institute of Gerontology
King's College London

Published May 1996
London: HMSO

ISBN 0 11 321966 0

Foreword

We all know that people mostly live longer now than they used to. It follows that the post-retirement phase of their lives forms a substantial part of the whole story, almost certainly longer than childhood and adolescence. We must learn not to lump everyone together, once they have retired, as 'the elderly', nor think of them as Shakespeare's slippered pantaloons and toothless crones. Everybody ages at a different rate, but there is much to be said for subdividing 'the third age' into those who are between sixty and eighty, and those who are older. Those who fall into the first category (and indeed some of the others) are for the most part energetic, active and interested in a wide variety of things; they are people whose talents ought not to be wasted.

I greatly welcome this volume, the second from the Gerontology Data Service. It explores the diversity of the older population through an examination of how active people are: at home, with their families and friends, and in their communities.

Through new analyses of national survey data it sheds light on the energy and participation of most of those who have retired. Yet it also reminds us that, at the other end, the very old are almost necessarily dependent, and that some live extremely narrow and restricted lives.

Baroness Mary Warnock

Acknowledgements

The financial support of **Age Concern England**, which enabled the development of the Gerontology Data Service, is gratefully acknowledged.

Material from the **General Household Survey** and the Office of Population Censuses and Surveys' (OPCS) **Surveys of Disability in Great Britain**, made available through OPCS and The Data Archive, has been used by permission of the controller of HMSO.

Material from the **Family Expenditure Surveys** is Crown copyright and has been made available by the Central Statistical Office through The Data Archive and used by permission of the controller of HMSO.

Material from the **British Social Attitudes Survey** was made available by Social and Community Planning Research through The Data Archive.

Material from the **Survey of Retirement and Retirement Plans** was made available directly from OPCS and has been used by permission of the Controller of HMSO.

Neither the depositing bodies nor The Data Archive bears any responsibility for the analysis or interpretation of the data reported here.

Material from the **International Passenger Survey** was commissioned in the form of tabulations from the Statistics Division of the Department of National Heritage.

Material from the **National Travel Survey** was commissioned in the form of tabulations from the Statistics Division of the Department of Transport. Neither of these Departments bears any responsibility for the analysis or interpretation of the data reported here.

Local Base Statistics from the **1991 Census of Population** have been reproduced with the permission of the Controller of HMSO and are Crown copyright.

We are grateful to other colleagues at the Institute who have helped with this Report, especially Linda Murgatroyd who worked on it in its early stages.

Contents

Chapter 4   Getting around the home

Key facts – Independence at home – The home itself – General health – Personal care – Domestic tasks – Getting around the home – Help from other people – Special facilities, machines or gadgets

Chapter 6   Getting around outside the home
Key facts – Getting around the neighbourhood – Going further afield – Getting around with a disability   69

Chapter 7   Summary

Appendix A

Introduction

The Gerontology Data Service at the Age Concern Institute of Gerontology, King's College London

The Age Concern Institute of Gerontology (ACIOG) at King's College London was set up by Age Concern England and King's College in 1986. Its overall aims are to foster the understanding of ageing and old age and to develop the means of improving the well-being of older people. Britain's ageing population has social, economic and political implications, and means that detailed, up-to-date information on the older population is needed by policy makers, service planners, the providers of goods and services, as well as by researchers, students and teachers. It was with this in mind that ACIOG developed the Gerontology Data Service (GDS) to provide analysis and interpretation of data in reports such as this, and customised analyses for specific clients on subjects of particular relevance to the study of older people.

Profiles of Britain's older population

A major aim of the GDS is to bridge some of the gaps in the published tabulations of government survey data by providing information focused specifically on older people in a series of regular reports. Our first report, *Life After 60* (Askham et al., 1992) provided a general profile of Britain's older population, with chapters covering living arrangements, housing and household amenities, finances, employment and retirement, health and leisure. It was not intended to be comprehensive and many aspects of the lives of elderly people could not be included; the report did, however, illustrate well the impressive range of previously unpublished data available from government surveys. All subsequent reports will have different special themes. **At the same time, however, each report will update key material from the previous report.**

Getting Around After Sixty

The current report has a special focus, getting around in later life. We chose this theme for a number of reasons, partly as a contribution to the dispelling of myths about later life as inevitably a time of *in*activity, partly because it is a topic of particular current interest, with the *Health of the Nation* (Secretary of State for Health, 1992) targets emphasising the importance for health of remaining active, partly because much of the existing evidence about the physical activity levels of older people is confined to a restricted range of pastimes such as sport, rather than to the wider array of physically active pursuits involved in work, personal business, leisure, domestic life, caregiving, etc. By putting them together we hope to present a richer picture of the various ways, and the extent to which, older people get around. A final reason for the choice of this topic is to do with data availability: we wanted to disseminate material about older people from the OPCS Surveys of Disability in Britain before it became outdated.

This volume therefore looks at aspects of employment in later life, leisure, helping others, and independence inside and outside the home. Parts of Chapters Three, Four and Six focus on the particular problems faced by disabled elderly people (nearly half of the estimated six million disabled adults in Great Britain are aged 70 and over; Martin et al., 1988:pxii, and 50% of the population aged 70 and over is disabled). Certain tables in the main text are noted as updates of previous tables in *Life After 60;* on the whole, however, updated tables will be found in Appendix A. These are tables on population, living arrangements, general health, disability and housing, which are of general interest but of less relevance to the special theme of the report, and have not been published elsewhere. These will be updated in each new report. It is hoped that, in this way, we will in time build up a useful series on the diverse and changing aspects of life in old age.

Data sources The main sources used in *Life After 60* were the continuous government surveys carried out by the Office of Population Censuses and Surveys (OPCS): the General Household Survey and the Family Expenditure Survey. Our emphasis in this report remains with the General Household Survey, and in particular with the General Household Survey of 1991. The main reason for this is the particular relevance to our theme, getting around in later life, of the special module of that year on people aged 65 and over. The module asked questions about a wide range of tasks important for independent living; for example, questions on levels of difficulty with personal care, domestic and locomotive tasks (see Goddard and Savage, 1994, for further information). Chapters Four, Five and Six all draw heavily on questions in the special module to examine aspects of getting around the home, getting around outside the home, and getting around for others. Since *Life After 60,* the 1991 Census of Population has become available and is used in this report. Thus in order to standardize the date to which data refer, we have chosen 1991 whenever we could, even if this was not the most up-to-date material available.

However, a major aim of the GDS is to provide access to a wide and expanding data base of survey information, and in this report we add information from the Survey of Retirement and Retirement Plans (carried out in late 1988 and early 1989) and the OPCS Surveys of Disability in Great Britain, which were carried out in 1985 and 1986 and contain the most up-to-date nationally representative information on disabled people. Appendix B provides an easy reference guide to all the surveys and sources used in this report, which will, like Appendix A, be updated and expanded in subsequent reports.

Methodological issues Some difficulties in interpreting sample survey data were emphasised in *Life After 60* (Askham et al, 1992:p13–15). In particular, the following should be noted:

- there is particular difficulty with cross-sectional data in distinguishing between age and cohort effects. Differences between age groups may reflect either 'true' ageing effects, or differences in life experiences between different cohorts, or both. In the absence of longitudinal data, it is very difficult to know which.

- all results are subject to sampling error. The sample may differ in behaviour and characteristics from the true underlying population (see Appendix C for calculation of sampling error). In some cases sample sizes may be so small, and the corresponding confidence intervals so large, that the presentation of data is almost meaningless. In the tables in the following chapters, figures from sample sizes of under 50 are bracketed; any statistics associated with sample sizes this small should be regarded with extreme caution. Problems associated with small sample sizes are particularly evident in Chapter Four, where we see that men aged 90 and over find it easier to do several tasks than men aged 85–89 (for example, 75% of men aged 90 and over found it 'not difficult' to wash themselves all over, compared with only 54% of men aged 85-89, **Table 4.4**). Although it is possible to hypothesise, for example, that it is only the 'super-fit' who are able to survive to 90, it would be unwise to do so; the sample size is only 24 men. However, we do present data on people aged 90 and over, because of the considerable current interest in this age group.

For further information about the service and publications of the GDS, you are invited to contact Dr. Claire Jarvis, Gerontology Data Service, ACIOG, King's College London, Cornwall House, Waterloo Road, London SE1 8WA.

2

Getting Around for Work

Some key facts*

- 18% of men aged 60 and over were in paid employment and 8% of women (this fell to 9% of men and 4% of women aged 65 and over).

- the trend towards earlier retirement for men has continued; 30% of men aged 60–64 were retired compared with 23% three years earlier.

- in contrast, more older women go out to work than used to be the case; 22% of women aged 60–64 were working compared with 19% three years earlier.

- older workers work shorter hours than younger people, especially over state pension age; over that age half the men worked for no more than 30 hours a week, and a third of the women worked for no more than 15 hours a week.

- people of 60 and over travelled on average 240 miles a year to and from work in 1989/91, whereas those under 60 travelled 1,550 miles.

- amongst older married couples, where one of the partners is still working it is almost as likely to be the wife as the husband; in the age group 60–64 12% of married women were sole earners in the marriage and 15% of married men.

- older men in employment were more likely to have jobs in distribution and catering, or agriculture, fishing and food and less likely than men under the age of 65 to work in manufacturing or construction.

- older employed women were somewhat more likely to have jobs in distribution and catering and other services than women under the age of 60 (though these were the most common sectors of work for women of all ages) and somewhat less likely to work in banking and finance.

- mean weekly income from employment over state pension age was only £13 for men and £6 for women.

---

* All figures relate to 1991 and to Great Britain unless otherwise stated, and exclude people living in institutions.

3

For many people their work is an important reason for getting out and about. Most of us with jobs take the change of scenery and company that work provides for granted and are perhaps more inclined to dwell on the problems of getting to and from work. The cessation from work when retirement comes leaves a significant hole, welcome or otherwise, in this part of daily life. Work also generates income which affects how much one can afford to spend on travel (amongst other things). Retired people may have more time for travel, but are likely to have less money available for it than younger people.

In this chapter we look at a number of aspects of employment in later life. We start by establishing how participation in paid work varies across age groups with particular reference to people aged 60 or more. We look at the industries in which older people are employed and at the hours they work. This chapter also includes some analysis of the contribution in later life, of employment income to personal and household income.

Employment in later life   Although later life is generally a time of retirement from paid work, some 18% of men aged 60 and over and eight per cent of women were in employment or self-employment in 1991 (**Table 2.1** and **Figures 2.1 and 2.2**).

Table 2.1 Employment status, by age group and gender, Great Britain, 1991

	16–24 years	25–34 years	35–44 years	45–54 years	55–59 years	60–64 years	65–69 years	70–74 years	75–79 years	80 yrs and over	under 60 years	women under 60, men under 65	60 yrs and over	women 60 yrs & over, men 65 yrs & over
	%	%	%	%	%	%	%	%	%	%	%	%	%	%
Men														
employee	60	72	71	69	52	33	10	4	2	1	67	65	13	5
self-employed	5	13	16	15	15	9	5	4	3	2	13	12	5	4
unemployed	15	8	6	6	9	5	0	0	0	0	9	8	1	0
sick	1	2	3	6	13	18	2	0	1	1.	4	5	6	1
retired	0	0	0	1	7	30	82	91	92	95	1	3	73	89
other	19	5	3	3	4	4	1	1	2	2	7	6	2	1
N (base)	924	1,277	1,126	993	401	395	392	303	221	176	4,721	5,116	1,487	1,092
Women														
employee	61	61	67	64	48	20	6	2	1	0	62		7	
self-employed	1	5	6	5	3	2	2	0	1	0	4		1	
unemployed	6	4	2	4	3	0	0	0	0	0	4		0	
sick	2	2	3	5	7	2	1	1	0	0	3		1	
retired	0	0	0	1	10	51	71	77	75	68	1		68	
other	29	28	21	21	29	25	20	20	24	32	25		24	
N (base)	997	1,336	1,147	966	405	466	466	390	343	328	4,851		1,993	
Men and Women														
employee	61	66	69	67	50	26	8	3	1	0	65	63	9	6
self-employed	3	9	11	10	9	5	3	2	1	1	9	9	3	2
unemployed	11	6	4	5	6	3	0	0	0	0	6	6	1	0
sick	2	2	3	6	10	9	1	0	0	0	3	4	3	1
retired	0	0	0	1	8	41	76	83	81	77	1	2	70	75
other	24	17	12	12	17	15	11	12	15	21	16	16	14	16
N (base)	1,921	2,613	2,273	1,959	806	861	858	693	564	504	9,572	9,967	3,480	3,085

Source: Family Expenditure Survey 1991

Figure 2.1 Employment status of men, by age group, Great Britain, 1991

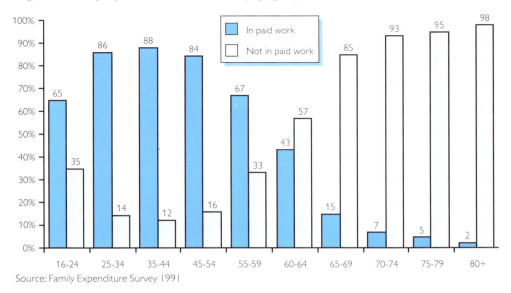

Source: Family Expenditure Survey 1991

Figure 2.2 Employment status of women, by age group, Great Britain, 1991

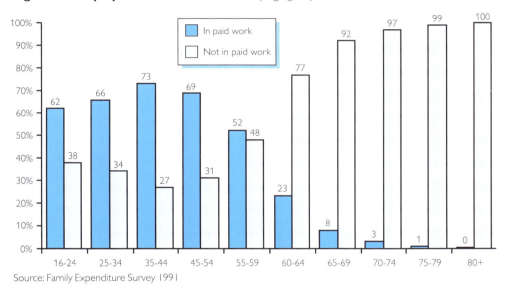

Source: Family Expenditure Survey 1991

In the age group 60–64 years, two-fifths of men and between a fifth and a quarter of women were getting around for work[1]. Some five per cent of men aged 60–64 and three per cent of women in the same age group were unemployed: they wanted a job but did not have one.

---

[1]**Some may in fact be working from home. The 1991 Census of Population recorded 5% of all employees and self-employed people aged 16 and over as working 'mainly from home' (Felstead and Jewson, 1995).**

It is well known that there has been a trend amongst men towards early retirement, whether voluntary or involuntary. In 1991, 30% of men aged 60–64 were retired compared with just 23% three years earlier (Askham et al, 1992:p87). The trend towards early retirement also means that amongst the retired, older men will tend to have retired later than younger men. This is illustrated in **Figure 2.3.**

Figure 2.3 Age retired, retired men aged 65 and over, Great Britain, 1991

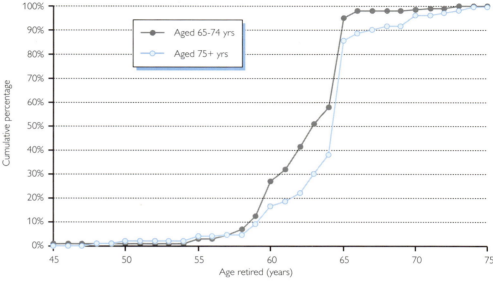

Source: British Social Attitudes Survey 1991

This figure plots the cumulative proportions of retired men aged at least 65 years, who had retired by each age (between the ages of 45 and 75). Separate graphs are shown for men aged under and over 75 years. The vertical distance between the top line (which relates to the younger generation of retired men) and the lower line (which refers to the older generation), indicates the extent to which more of the younger generation had retired at each age. Thus 27% of those currently aged 65–74 had retired by the time they were 60 compared with only 16% of the group of men now aged over 75. By age 64, nearly 60% of the younger cohort had retired, compared with 38% of the older age group.

In contrast to the trend towards early retirement by men, more women go out to work than used to be the case. In the age group 60–64, 22% of women were in paid work in 1991, compared with 19% in 1988. As a result of higher labour force participation among women, more seem to class themselves as 'retired' in later life rather than 'not working'. In 1991 the proportion of women aged 60 and over who regarded themselves as retired was 68%, compared with 62% in 1988 (Askham et al, 1992:p87).

If we compare men and women who are within five years of reaching their respective state pension ages, women are much more likely to be in work than men. More than one woman in five (22%) aged 60–64 years was in work, compared with 15% of men aged 65–69. For women this figure is a little higher than in 1988, when it stood at 18.6% (Askham et al, 1992:p55).

It is clear from these figures that there must be much less travelling for work among older people than among younger people. **Table 2.2** compares distances travelled for commuting and business by older and younger people, based on the National Travel Survey of 1989/1991.

Table 2.2 Distance travelled per year for commuting, business and all purposes, by age group and gender, Great Britain

	under 60 years*	60–64 years	65–69 years	70–74 years	75–79 years	80–84 years	85–89 years	90 years and over	60 years and over
Average per year(miles)									
Men									
commuting	2,243	1,287	313	102	114	9	0	–	**466**
business	1,459	999	166	108	10	9	82	–	**336**
total	8,382	6,358	5,485	3,807	3,619	2,106	2,013	–	**4,726**
N (base)	10,154	660	697	478	396	184	69	(13)	**2,497**
Women									
commuting	872	169	52	48	11	2	0	0	**62**
business	258	50	42	5	15	1	0	0	**25**
total	5,753	4,432	3,985	3,201	2,174	1,729	754	(413)	**3,171**
N (base)	10,399	742	780	575	578	367	146	(47)	**3,235**
Per cent of total miles travelled	%	%	%	%	%	%	%	%	%
Men									
commuting	26.8	20.2	5.7	2.7	3.2	0.4	0.0	–	**9.9**
business	17.4	15.7	3.0	2.8	0.3	0.4	4.1	–	**7.1**
Women									
commuting	15.2	3.8	1.3	1.5	0.5	0.1	0.0	0.0	**2.0**
business	4.5	1.1	1.1	0.2	0.7	0.1	0.0	0.0	**0.8**

Source: National Travel Survey 1989/91, unpublished data, commissioned from Department of Transport, Statistics Division

Notes: *   includes those aged under 16
         –   sample size too small for reliable estimate
         ( )   based on small numbers; should be used with caution

The average number of commuting miles per year travelled by people aged under 60 (including children) was more than six times that for older people (1,549 miles compared with 238 miles), although in total older people travelled over 50% as many miles as younger people on average. Whereas over a fifth of all miles travelled by those aged under 60 involved journeys to or from work, and another 12% were in the course of other journeys undertaken for business, the corresponding proportions for older people were just six per cent and four per cent (see Chapter 3).

Over the age of 60, the total number of miles travelled for commuting to and from work falls steadily with age, but remains markedly lower for women than for men, even above the age of 70 years (**Figures 2.4 and 2.5**). There is a surprising increase in business travel for men between the ages of 85 and 89 but this is probably due to sampling error: the sample size is only 69.

Figure 2.4 Average distance travelled per year for commuting and business by men, by age group, men aged 60 and over, Great Britain

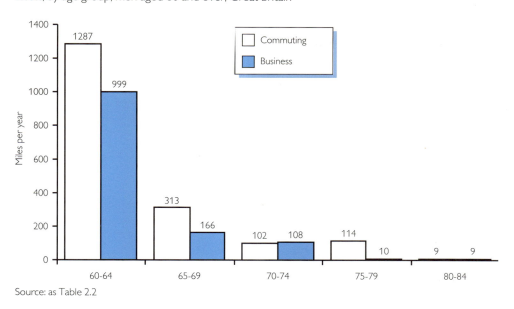

Source: as Table 2.2

Figure 2.5 Average distance travelled per year for commuting and business by women, by age group, women aged 60 and over, Great Britain

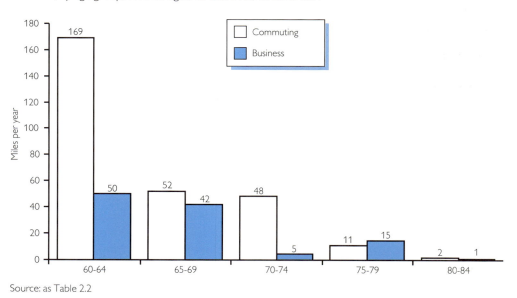

Source: as Table 2.2

For married people, the consequences of retirement from paid work depend to some extent on the employment status of their partners. If both are retired, they may have more time for joint leisure activities but perhaps less money for holidays and so forth. Evidence from the 1988 Survey of Retirement and Retirement Plans shows that women, in particular, quite often choose to time their retirement to coincide with that of their husbands. Eleven per cent of women who had retired early or were expecting to retire early, did so in order to retire at the same time as their husbands. Fifteen per cent of women who had retired late or expected to retire late, did so for this reason. Eight per cent of women who had not worked or did not expect to work beyond the normal retirement age said they did/would not, so that they could retire at the same time as their husbands (Bone et al,1992:p56).

Table 2.3 shows the combined employment states of married or cohabiting men and women, by age group, for 1991.

Table 2.3 Employment status of partners, by age group and gender, of all married/cohabiting individuals, Great Britain, 1991

	16–24 years	25–54 years	55–59 years	60–64 years	65–69 years	70–74 years	75 yrs & over	under 60 years	60 yrs & over	women under 60, men under 65	women 60 yrs & over, men 65 yrs & over
	%	%	%	%	%	%	%	%	%	%	%
Men											
both in paid work	64	66	48	40	4	2	1	**64**	**13**	**62**	**2**
in paid work, partner not	15	23	25	15	9	6	4	**23**	**9**	**22**	**7**
not in work, partner in work	5	4	10	21	12	6	5	**5**	**12**	**6**	**8**
neither in work	16	7	17	25	74	86	91	**8**	**66**	**10**	**83**
N (base)	236	2,615	331	320	304	225	244	**3,182**	**1,093**	**3,502**	**773**
Women											
both in paid work	60	65	36	10	4	1	1	**62**	**5**		
in paid work, partner not	5	5	17	12	6	2	0	**6**	**6**		
not in work, partner in work	22	22	22	19	10	5	6	**22**	**12**		
neither in work	13	8	24	58	80	92	93	**10**	**78**		
N (base)	395	2,657	310	298	276	183	156	**3,362**	**913**		
Men and Women											
both in paid work	61	66	42	26	4	1	1	**63**	**9**	**62**	**4**
in paid work, partner not	9	14	21	13	8	4	2	**14**	**8**	**14**	**6**
not in work, partner in work	15	13	16	20	11	6	5	**14**	**12**	**14**	**10**
neither in work	14	7	20	41	77	89	92	**9**	**71**	**10**	**80**
N (base)	631	5,272	641	618	580	408	400	**6,544**	**2,006**	**6,864**	**1,686**

Source: Family Expenditure Survey 1991

Amongst men aged 60 and over, 13% were in work and had partners who were also in work. Twelve per cent were not in work themselves but had partners who were. Two-thirds of married or cohabiting men aged 60 and over were not in work and had wives who were also not working. Over state pension age, the proportion in this situation rises to 83%. These figures are in stark contrast to the pattern amongst younger men. In the age group 55–59, nearly a half of married men were in work and had partners who were also working. Of those ten years older, only four per cent were in this position.

Looking at the situation from the perspective of women, the proportion of married women aged 60 and over who were in work and had partners in work was only five per cent. A similar percentage (six per cent) were in work but had partners who were not. It is noticeable that in the age group 60–64, the proportion of married men and women who were 'sole breadwinners' (they were in work but their partners were not) were quite similar (15% and 12% respectively). At all younger age groups, the proportion of men who were sole earners far exceeded the proportion of women who were in this situation. Thus for women, later life can be a time when they are going out to work, leaving a 'house-husband' at home. Taking married men and women together, seven out of ten of those aged 60 and over are in the situation where neither partner is in work; over state pension age this rises to eight out of ten.

There are some notable differences in the industries in which older and younger people work (**Table 2.4**).

Table 2.4 Industrial sector worked in, by age group and gender, of employees and self-employed people, Great Britain, 1991

	16–19 years	20–29 years	30–44 years	45–64 years	16–64 years	65 yrs & over	all ages
	%	%	%	%	%	%	%
Men							
Agriculture, fishing & food	3	2	2	3	3	10	3
Energy & water	1	2	3	3	3	0	3
Mining	2	3	4	4	4	2	4
Manufacturing, metal etc.	11	12	13	14	13	8	13
Manufacturing, other	10	10	9	9	9	8	9
Construction	14	13	12	12	12	7	12
Distribution & catering	34	20	16	15	17	24	18
Transport	4	8	9	10	9	5	9
Banking & finance	8	13	12	10	11	15	11
Other services	12	16	20	19	19	21	19
Women							
Agriculture, fishing & food	1	1	1	1	1	3	1
Energy & water	1	1	1	1	1	0	1
Mining	1	2	1	2	2	1	2
Manufacturing, metal etc.	4	5	4	5	4	3	4
Manufacturing, other	9	9	7	8	8	6	8
Construction	2	1	2	2	2	2	2
Distribution & catering	38	23	23	24	24	28	25
Transport	3	4	3	3	3	2	3
Banking & finance	17	19	13	9	14	9	13
Other services	24	35	45	47	41	46	41

Source: 1991 Census of Population, Local Base Statistics (10% sample)

In the context of this report it is interesting to see that the proportion of working men under state pension age who work in the transport sector is nearly double the proportion of older working men. Nearly a quarter of working men aged over state pension age worked in distribution and catering. This proportion was second only to the equivalent proportion for men aged 16–19. Thus young and old are to be found disproportionately in this sector. The other striking fact is that men over state pension age were more than three times as likely as younger men to be in agriculture, fishing or food industries.

In all age groups, women were highly concentrated in 'other services', which include, for example, public administration, education, health services, personal and domestic services. In all but the youngest age groups this was the most common employment sector for women. Forty-six per cent of women aged 60 and over were working in this sector. Although only very small proportions of women of all ages worked in agriculture, fishing and food, like men, women over state pension age were far more likely than younger women to have jobs in this sector. Again like men, the oldest and youngest women were particularly likely to work in distribution and catering, although this was a common sector for women of all ages.

Figures 2.6 and 2.7 show the proportions of each industry's male and female workforce which are accounted for by older workers. In each figure the vertical arrow marks the proportion of total workforce accounted for by older workers. Horizontal bars which stop to the left of this arrow indicate an industry where older workers are under-represented; bars which finish to the right of the arrow identify industries where older workers are over-represented.

Figure 2.6 Proportion of male employees who are aged 65 years and over, by industry, Great Britain, 1991

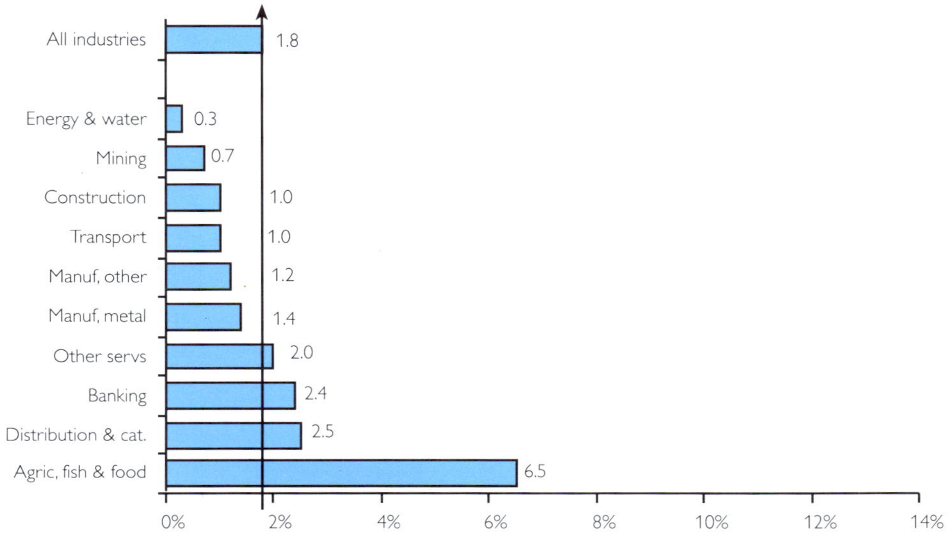

Source: 1991 Census of Population, Local Base Statistics (10% sample)

Men aged 65 and over account for slightly less than two per cent of all employees. But in agriculture, fishing and food they make up more than six per cent of all employees. Similarly they are disproportionately employed in distribution and catering, banking and other services, and are under-represented in all other sectors. Women aged 60 or more account for just over four per cent of all employees. However, they make up more than 12% of employees in the agricultural, fishing and food sector, and are also slightly over-represented relative to all women aged over 60, in distribution and catering; construction and other services. Unlike men over pension age, women over pension age are under-represented in banking and finance.

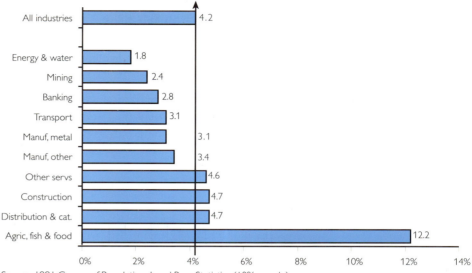

Figure 2.7 Proportion of female employees who are aged 60 years and over, by industry, Great Britain, 1991

Source: 1991 Census of Population, Local Base Statistics (10% sample)

When in work, older people tend to work fewer hours per week than younger people (**Table 2.5 and Figures 2.8 and 2.9**). Whereas 90% of working men aged under 60 worked at least 35 hours per week, less than three-quarters of men aged 60 and over worked for more than 35 hours a week and 14% worked for fewer than 22 hours a week. Beyond state pension age, although 42% worked for more than 35 hours per week, the majority worked for no more than 30 hours a week, and over a fifth worked for fewer than 16 hours a week.

Table 2.5 Weekly hours worked, by age group and gender, of employees and self-employed, Great Britain, 1991

Number of hours worked:	under 60 yrs	60 yrs & over	65 yrs & over	Number of hours worked:	under 60 yrs	60 yrs & over	65 yrs & over
	%	%	%		%	%	%
Men				**Women**			
3 and under	0.1	0.5	1.3	3 and under	0.5	2.0	3.4
4–7	0.3	1.6	4.5	4–7	2.9	7.7	11.5
8–15	1.0	6.2	16.8	8–15	11.6	25.0	30.5
16–21	0.7	6.1	15.1	16–21	12.5	19.2	18.4
22–23	0.1	0.7	1.6	22–23	1.9	2.9	2.1
24–30	1.7	6.4	13.1	24–30	10.7	13.6	12.5
31–35	6.7	5.8	5.9	31–35	12.8	7.2	5.2
36–40	63.2	52.5	25.3	36–40	40.3	17.3	10.9
41–50	16.9	13.2	9.3	41–50	4.7	2.8	2.8
51–60	5.9	4.0	3.9	51–60	1.1	1.0	1.2
61 and over	3.6	2.9	3.2	61 and over	1.0	1.3	1.5
Total	100.0	100.0	100.0	Total	100.0	100.0	100.0

Source: 1991 Census of Population, Local Base Statistics (10% sample)

Figure 2.8 Weekly hours worked by employed and self-employed men, men aged under and over 60 years, Great Britain, 1991

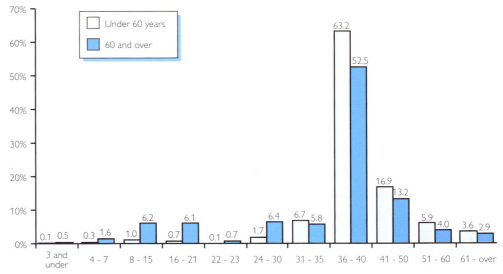

Source: 1991 Census of Population, Local Base Statistics (10% sample)

Figure 2.9 Weekly hours worked by employed and self-employed women, women aged under and over 60 years, Great Britain, 1991

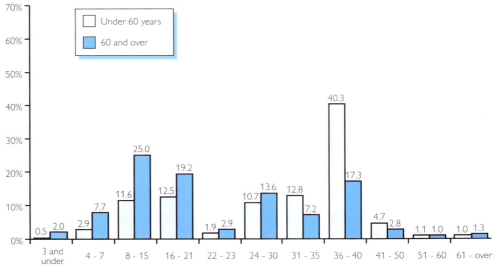

Source: 1991 Census of Population, Local Base Statistics (10% sample)

At all ages women are more likely to work part time than men. However, women who work beyond the age of 60 are particularly likely to work for only a few hours a week. In 1991, over a third of women aged 60 and over who worked, worked for no more than 15 hours a week.

Income Because they are less likely to have jobs, on average, of course, older people receive much less of their incomes in the form of income from employment or self-employment, than younger people. When they do work they are also more likely to work part-time as we have already seen, and they may receive lower rates of pay. In 1991, the average weekly gross earned income of men under 60 was £266 (in today's prices[2]); amongst men aged 75 years and over, gross earned income averaged just £2 a week (**Table 2.6**).

Table 2.6 Contribution of employment income, by age and gender, Great Britain, 1991

	under 60 yrs	60–64 yrs	65–69 yrs	70–74 yrs	75 yrs & over	60 yrs & over	men 65 yrs & over
Men							
Mean gross weekly income from	£266	£111	£29	£9	£2	**£40**	**£13**
employment	(4.1)	(10.6)	(5.7)	(3.1)	(0.7)	**(3.4)**	**(2.3)**
Mean share of gross employment	79%	36%	7%	3%	1%	**12%**	**4%**
income in total income	(0.6)	(2.2)	(1.C)	(0.6)	(0.3)	**(0.8)**	**(0.4)**
Mean total net personal income	£220	£192	£164	£157	£127	**£160**	**£149**
	(3.4)	(10.1)	(6.4)	(8.7)	(6.7)	**(4.1)**	**(4.1)**
Median total net personal income	£196	£162	£127	£115	£91	**£120**	**£109**
	(0.7)	(3.4)	(2.2)	(3.1)	(2.3)	**(1.0)**	**(1.1)**
Mean total net household income	£180	£162	£142	£142	£124	**£143**	**£136**
adjusted for household composition	(2.4)	(7.0)	(4.7)	(7.3)	(5.0)	**(3.0)**	**(3.2)**
Median total net household income	£157	£142	£114	£109	£94	**£114**	**£109**
adjusted for household composition	(0.5)	(2.4)	(1.6)	(2.7)	(1.7)	**(0.8)**	**(1.1)**
N (base)							
for average/median income levels	4,721	395	392	303	397	**1,487**	**1,092**
for share	4,606	394	392	303	396	**1,485**	**1,091**
Women							
Mean gross weekly income from	£109	£23	£5	£2	£0	**£6**	
employment	(1.8)	(2.6)	(1.2)	(0.9)	(0.1)	**(0.7)**	
Mean share of gross employment	59%	14%	3%	1%	0%	**0%**	
income in total income	(0.6)	(1.4)	(0.6)	(0.3)	(0.1)	**(0)**	
Mean total net personal income	£113	£94	£80	£82	£87	**£86**	
	(1.6)	(3.6)	(3.2)	(3.5)	(2.4)	**(1.5)**	
Median total net personal income	£94	£70	£64	£62	£66	**£66**	
	(0.3)	(1.2)	(1.0)	(1.2)	(0.7)	**(0.4)**	
Mean total net household income	£179	£159	£135	£124	£114	**£132**	
adjusted for household composition	(2.4)	(4.6)	(4.2)	(4.6)	(3.7)	**(2.2)**	
Median total net household income	£157	£140	£111	£92	£84	**£132**	
adjusted for household composition	(0.5)	(1.5)	(1.4)	(1.5)	(1.1)	**(2.2)**	
N (base)							
for average/median income levels	4,851	466	466	390	671	**1,993**	
for share	4,698	452	466	390	666	**1,974**	

Source: Family Expenditure Survey 1991

Note: standard errors in brackets

---

[2]**April 1995 prices, using the Retail Price Index.**

Below the age of 60 years, men received on average nearly 80% of their gross personal income from earnings. In the age group 60 to 64 years, earnings contributed an average of little more than a third of total income and they accounted for just one per cent of the income of men aged 75 years and over. Similarly, younger women received more in income from employment than older women. At £23 per week, the average level of earned income of women aged 60–64 years was just a fifth of that of younger women. Above the age of 64 women's incomes from employment were very small indeed.

There are pronounced differences between the levels of earned incomes of men and women. This is because women have lower rates of participation in work, are more likely to work part-time and have lower rates of pay. The differences between men's and women's employment incomes are greater over than under the age of 60. The average earned income of women under 60 was about 40% of that of men aged under 60. At older ages, women's earned incomes average a fifth or less of men's.

When people retire, their earnings are typically replaced by pensions of various kinds. However, pensions are almost invariably lower than the earnings they replace and this is apparent from the fact that total personal income also falls with age beyond retirement. In 1991, the average net personal income of men aged under 60 was £220 per week. The average income of men aged 75 years or more was £127, which is less than 60% of the average income of men under 60. Average incomes are not necessarily the best indicators of income levels. An alternative and in many respects more representative measure is median income (Hancock and Weir, 1994). The median income is the mid-point of the income distribution: 50% of people have incomes above it and 50% below it. Median total income levels are almost always substantially lower than average income levels because they are less influenced by the very high incomes of a few people. So for example, the median net personal income of men aged 60 and over was only £120 a week, compared with £160 for the average. Furthermore, the gap between older and younger men's median incomes was larger than the gap between their average incomes. The average income of men aged 60 and over was nearly three-quarters (73%) of the average income of men aged under 60, but their median income was only 61% of younger men's median income.

Women's total income also falls with age. However, at age groups above 60–64 there is not a great deal of difference in median incomes, whereas for men incomes fall steadily with age (**Figure 2.10**). This is partly due to growth in occupational pension coverage which is an important reason for the difference between the incomes of younger and older generations of retired men but has as yet had less effect on the personal incomes of retired women. Differences between the incomes of older and younger women tend to be smaller for women than for men. For example, in 1991 the median income of women aged over 60 years was only 30% below that of younger women, whereas the equivalent gap for men was nearly 40%.

Figure 2.10 Median personal net weekly income, by age and gender, Great Britain, 1991

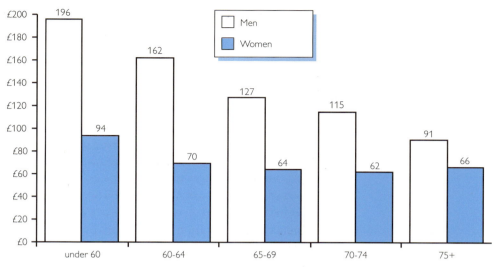

Source: Family Expenditure Survey 1991

As with earned income, differences between men's and women's total net personal incomes are generally larger in proportionate terms than the gaps between older and younger women's incomes. However, differences between the incomes of men and women are smaller at older ages than at younger ages (**Figure 2.11**). Below the age of 60, the median income of women is just under a half (48%) that of men. This percentage falls to 43% in the age group 60–64, largely because more women than men are retired at this stage, but rises again at older ages, reaching 72% for those aged 75 and over.

Figure 2.11 The median net personal income of women as a proportion of that of men in the same group, by age group, Great Britain, 1991

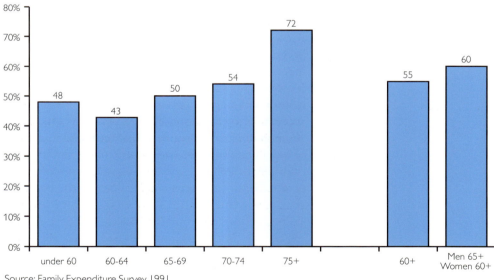

Source: Family Expenditure Survey 1991

The way in which personal income varies with age reflects a combination of age and cohort (or generation) effects. An example of the first is the reduction in income which accompanies retirement. This has occurred for all people who are currently retired and is probably the most important reason why income levels amongst older people in general are lower than they are for younger people. Incomes may also fall during retirement if, for example, pensions in payment are not increased to compensate fully for rising prices. This is one reason why incomes are lower amongst older retired people than amongst the more recently retired. Growth in occupational pensions which occurred in the 1950s, 60s and 70s (see for example, Government Actuary, 1994) is an example of a trend which has cohort effects. It manifests itself in higher incomes amongst younger pensioners than amongst older pensioners because more of the recently retired have substantial occupational pensions. However, in time, as today's younger pensioners age, the proportion of older pensioners with occupational pensions will rise and the difference between the incomes of older and younger pensioners can be expected to decrease. Similarly, increased participation in paid work by women means that younger women pensioners are more likely to have pensions in their own right and produces higher average incomes for today's younger retired women than for older retired women, but again this gap will decrease in time.

Low personal income can be mitigated by financial support from other family or household members. On the other hand, one person's income often has to support more than one person. Thus a low (or high) personal income may not indicate a low (or high) standard of living. There is, rightly, a good deal of debate as to whether it is justified to assume that all members of a household share equally in the household's total income. Evidence exists that this is not always the case (see, for example, Pahl, 1990). Quite apart from the tangible things that an income affords, an income of one's own also brings less quantifiable benefits, such as independence. So household income is not necessarily a better guide to an individual's living standard than his or her personal income, but it is clearly important to take household income levels into account. Thus in **Table 2.6** we also show average and median total net household income levels, adjusted for household size[3]. This adjustment is designed to take into account the higher costs of living that larger households face but also their scope for reaping the benefits of economies of scale: two people living together can usually live more cheaply than if they had separate homes. Under the age of 60, the mean and median net household incomes of men and women were virtually identical in 1991. Average net household income was around £180 per week; median income levels were £157. In the age groups 60–64 and 65–69 the household income levels of men and women are quite close. However, at older ages a gap opens up with women living in poorer households than men. The main reason for this is that women tend to outlive their husbands and so at these ages are more likely to be living alone. Typically they inherit less than 100% of their husbands' pension rights. Thus even though they may have only themselves to support, the loss of economies of scale and at least some of their husbands' incomes leaves them generally poorer than men of the same age. For example, in 1991, the median weekly household income of women aged 70–74 was 15% (and £17) below that of men in the same age group. Over the age of 75, the gap was about 10% (although with a rather wide margin of error).

---

[3]**This is a scale of 1 for the first adult in the household, 0.7 for each subsequent adult or child aged 14 and over, and 0.5 for each child aged under 14 (sometimes referred to as the OECD Scale, although the OECD has used others as well).**

Getting Around For Leisure

Some key facts*

- the most common sedentary leisure pursuits in 1990 for people aged 60 and over were watching television (99%), listening to the radio (82%), and reading books (63%)

- in 1985 all disabled men and four fifths of disabled women aged 80 and over and living at home said that they sometimes sat for hours doing nothing; around a half found it hard to stir themselves to do something

- nearly four-fifths of all disabled men and women aged 60 and over and living at home did not regularly go anywhere for social activities in 1985

- gardening and 'do-it-yourself' are increasingly popular home-based physical activities among older people; for example in 1980 44% of people aged 70–74 had gardened in the past four weeks; in 1990 the figure was 57%

- walking was the most popular physical exercise among older people in 1990, with 40% of the men and 30% of the women aged 60 and over having been for a walk of two to five miles in the past four weeks

- however, a third of all men aged 60 and over, and a half of all women aged 60 and over, participated in no sporting activity at all in the past year in 1990

- older people without any long-standing illness are much more likely to take part in sporting activities; nonetheless in 1990 half the men with a limiting long-standing illness and a third of the women with such an illness had taken part in sporting activities in the previous year

- a quarter of people aged 60 and over in the UK lived in households which had paid for a holiday in the past three months in 1991; the proportion declined with age, especially for overseas holidays, and with income (though when asked, disabled people were more likely to mention disinclination or health rather than inability to afford it as the main reason for *not* taking a holiday)

---

* All figures relate to Great Britain unless otherwise stated and exclude people living in institutions

The picture of older people as jet–setting hedonists, pursuing pleasure around the globe is of course only applicable to a minority. However, leisure activities do not necessarily cost money (or not much) and any converse picture of elderly people too poor to *have* leisure pursuits is also obviously incorrect. If income level does affect leisure it may affect the kind of pursuits people can engage in more than the amount. (For example, poorer elderly people are much less likely to take holidays abroad than those in the highest income group; see **Table 3.9** below.) The same may well be true of the effect upon leisure of health (**Table 3.3**) or the nature of one's network of friends and relations.

Leisure activities are hard to define, with one man's gardening-for-fun being another's domestic chore or a third's physical exercise. Since we cannot here take subjective perceptions into account, leisure pursuits are defined as those generally seen as carried out for their own sakes, and for the pleasure obtained from the activity as much as for any outcomes achieved. They include sporting activities which may be carried out for their beneficial effects upon fitness as well as for pleasure.

Sedentary or indoor activities at home

A first and very obvious point is that older people (like people in other age groups) take a lot of their leisure activities sitting down at home; they do not have to do much 'getting about' to participate in them. In 1990 almost every adult had watched television in the preceding four weeks, regardless of age, sex or living arrangements (**Tables 3.1** and **3.2**).

Table 3.1 Leisure activities in the last four weeks, by age group and gender, Great Britain, 1990

	60–64 years	65–69 years	70–74 years	75–79 years	80–84 years	85–89 years	90 yrs & over	60 yrs & over	15–59 years
	%	%	%	%	%	%	%	%	%
Men									
watched tv	98	99	99	98	97	99	(91)	98	99
listened to radio	88	85	81	86	76	68	(64)	84	93
listened to records/tapes	70	61	55	48	37	28	(9)	57	86
read books	62	57	59	52	51	48	(27)	57	55
did gardening	65	64	67	55	47	47	(36)	62	49
did sewing/knitting	4	5	4	3	1	3	(0)	4	3
did DIY jobs	58	57	47	39	25	20	(9)	49	61
N (base)	579	568	415	273	158	75	(11)	2,079	5,984
Women									
watched tv	99	98	99	99	97	95	(95)	98	99
listened to radio	85	84	82	75	72	64	(56)	80	91
listened to records/tapes	65	58	44	35	26	23	(20)	47	86
read books	69	74	67	68	58	54	(51)	67	68
did gardening	54	53	49	37	30	19	(12)	45	44
did sewing/knitting	55	52	47	36	32	21	(10)	44	40
did DIY jobs	24	21	15	10	5	2	(2)	16	35
N (base)	624	656	523	459	292	146	(41)	2,741	6,677

Source: General Household Survey 1990

Note: ( ) Percentages in brackets are based on small numbers and should be used with caution

Similarly, the vast majority had listened to the radio, though the proportions were lower than for television, and declined with age (this decline being slightly more marked for women than men).

Table 3.2 Leisure activities in the last four weeks, by living arrangements, people aged 60 and over and 16–59, Great Britain, 1990

	Lives alone	Lives with spouse	Spouse and others	Others not spouse
	%	%	%	%
People aged 60 and over				
watched tv	97	99	100	99
listened to radio	78	85	82	75
listened to records/tapes	39	60	54	46
read books	66	64	56	55
did gardening	43	59	57	41
did sewing/knitting	33	24	20	30
did DIY jobs	18	37	43	20
N (base)	1,521	2,452	411	436
People aged 16–59				
watched tv	96	99	99	99
listened to radio	92	92	91	92
listened to records/tapes	83	84	84	90
read books	66	66	59	63
did gardening	40	58	53	25
did sewing/knitting	19	26	24	16
did DIY jobs	46	53	52	34
N (base)	956	2,623	5,888	3,194

Source: General Household Survey 1990

The third most common sedentary leisure pursuit for those aged 60 and over as a whole, and for which we have survey data, is reading books (nearly two-thirds had done so in the previous four weeks). Fifty per cent had listened to tapes or records. For men in their sixties, the latter pastime was more popular than reading, but for every other age group of older people, reading predominated. As one might expect, however, its occurrence declined with age so that, for example, although two-thirds of people aged 60–64 years had read books in the preceding four weeks, only half of those aged 85–89 years had done so. Women were slightly more likely to read than men. They were also much more likely to have sewed or knitted (44% as opposed to 4% of men aged 60 years and over), though this too declined with age. Those people aged 60 and over who lived alone were particularly unlikely, compared with those who lived with just a husband or wife, to have listened to tapes or records or the radio, but rather more likely to have knitted or sewed (this is because that group contains a higher proportion of women). There have been some slight increases in some of the sedentary activities since the 1987 General Household Survey (Askham et al, 1992, **Table 7.1**). For example, in 1987 46% said they had listened to tapes or records, and in 1990 it was 51%; in 1987 59% said they had read books, and in 1990 it was 63%.

We do not know much about the incidence of 'doing nothing', especially among the able-bodied, but we do know that high proportions of *dis*abled adults living in the community said they sometimes sit for hours doing nothing; for example, 100% of men over eighty years and four out of five women aged 80 and over agreed that this was how they spent much of their time (**Figure 3.1**; note, though, that the figures should be treated with caution as sample numbers are very small).

Figure 3.1 Disabled people who sometimes sit for hours doing nothing, by age group and gender, disabled people aged 60 and over and 16–59, living in private households, Great Britain, 1985

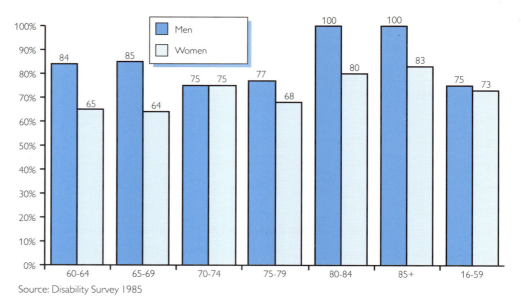

Source: Disability Survey 1985

In this they did not differ substantially from younger disabled adults, three-quarters of whom said they sometimes sat for hours doing nothing.

Indeed, just over a half of all these disabled people said they found it hard to stir themselves to do something. This feeling was higher in earlier late life (two-thirds reporting difficulty stirring themselves to do something) and dropped to about a half for those in their eighties (**Figure 3.2**).

Figure 3.2 Disabled people finding it hard to stir themselves to do something, by age group and gender, disabled people aged 60 and over and 16–59, living in private households, Great Britain, 1985

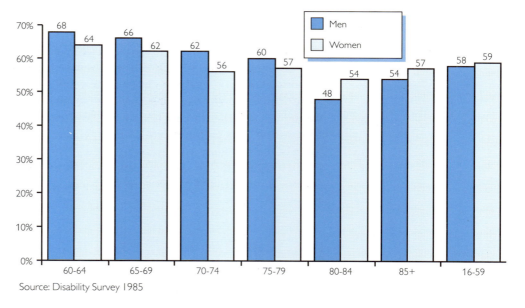

Source: Disability Survey 1985

This may reflect to some extent the different kinds of disability experienced by younger and older people. Although only small *proportions* of the general population are disabled, there are large *numbers* of disabled people living in private households. In 1985 there were estimated to be 5.8 million disabled adults living in the community (Martin et al, 1988: p16). As over one million of these were aged 80 and over (Martin et al, 1988: p18), and as they comprised two–thirds of the population then aged 80 and over, it follows that a high proportion of very old people spent a great deal of time just sitting doing nothing.

Physically active leisure pastimes at home or nearby

For home-based active pursuits we have survey data for gardening and 'do-it-yourself' (DIY) activities (**Table 3.1** above, and **Table 3.3**). As expected they show a gender, age and health bias. In 1990, three out of five men aged 60 and over had gardened in the previous month, and half had done DIY jobs; nearly a half of the women had also gardened and a sixth had done DIY jobs. For those with a limiting long-standing illness just over a half of the men – and a third of the women – had gardened, and two-fifths of the men and one in ten of the women had done DIY jobs.

Table 3.3 Leisure activities in past four weeks, by limiting long-standing illness and gender, people aged 60 and over, Great Britain, 1990

	Limiting long-standing illness	Non-limiting long-standing illness	No long-standing illness	All aged 60 & over
	%	%	%	%
Men				
watched tv	98	99	98	**98**
read books	53	64	59	**57**
did gardening	53	62	70	**61**
did DIY jobs	40	48	58	**49**
N (base)	852	393	830	**2,075**
Women				
watched tv	98	99	99	**98**
read books	63	72	70	**67**
did gardening	34	51	54	**45**
did DIY jobs	10	19	21	**16**
N (base)	1,167	526	1,036	**2,729**

Source: General Household Survey 1990

There was a steep decline in both of these active pastimes as people entered their seventies and beyond, but even so nearly a half of all men in their late eighties had gardened, as had one in five women. Unfortunately, because of the limitations of the data, it is not possible to exclude people who did not have a garden. However, if one examines only people living in a house or bungalow as a rough proxy for people with a garden, and looks only at people who were interviewed in the months April to September, when most gardening takes place, the proportions are quite substantial (four out of five men over sixty and two-thirds of women over sixty had gardened in the last four weeks; **Figure 3.3**).

Figure 3.3 People who did some gardening in the past four weeks, by age group and gender, people aged 60 and over who were interviewed between April and September and who lived in a house or bungalow, Great Britain, 1990

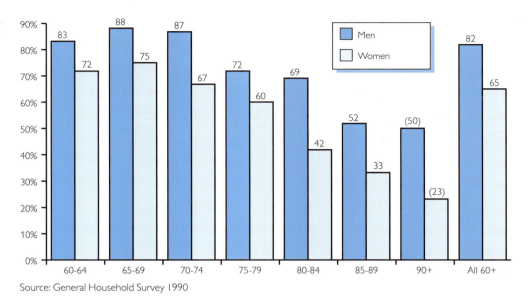

Source: General Household Survey 1990

One of the interesting things about these findings is the increase in activity since 1980 (see **Figure 3.4**) If this is a continuing trend, it supports the view that people are retaining more active lifestyles until later in their lives than used to be the case. The following graph compares 1980 with 1990 for those aged seventy and over.

Figure 3.4 People who did gardening and DIY in the past four weeks, by age group, people aged 70 and over, Great Britain, 1980 and 1990

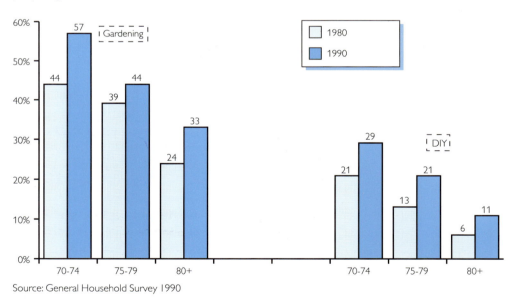

Source: General Household Survey 1990

Most older people get out and about for leisure purposes beyond their own homes and gardens. As far as walking or sport is concerned men are more active than women. For example, as **Table 3.4** shows, 70% of men over sixty (but only 50% of women) had participated in some sporting activity (including walking) in the past year. There was a steep decline with age for both men and women, but even so a third of the men over eighty and a fifth of the women had participated in some sporting activity in the past year.

Table 3.4 Sporting activities in the past year, by age group and gender, people aged 60 and over and 16–59, Great Britain, 1990

	60–64 years	65–69 years	70–74 years	75–79 years	80 yrs & over	60 yrs & over	16–59 years
	%	%	%	%	%	%	%
Men							
no physical exercise*	23	24	27	41	65	**31**	**6**
walk of 10 + miles	13	9	6	4	3	**8**	**19**
walk of 5–9 miles	35	30	27	18	9	**27**	**42**
walk of 2–5 miles	66	61	61	47	27	**57**	**72**
swimming	22	19	14	7	2	**15**	**53**
bowls	9	10	10	7	4	**8**	**7**
cycling	10	10	9	7	3	**9**	**25**
golf	10	9	6	6	2	**7**	**24**
keep fit	5	5	5	3	3	**5**	**10**
'passive' sport†	21	20	15	10	5	**16**	**54**
other 'active' sport‡	16	10	6	5	2	**9**	**62**
N (base)	582	572	419	273	245	**2,091**	**6,028**
Women							
no physical exercise*	27	38	50	65	81	**50**	**11**
walk of 10 + miles	8	5	3	2	0	**4**	**11**
walk of 5–9 miles	25	21	16	8	3	**16**	**33**
walk of 2–5 miles	61	53	43	30	15	**43**	**68**
swimming	21	18	7	3	1	**11**	**54**
bowls	6	5	3	1	1	**3**	**3**
cycling	9	5	4	1	0	**4**	**18**
golf	5	3	1	1	0	**2**	**7**
keep fit	14	11	7	5	2	**8**	**35**
'passive' sport†	5	3	2	2	1	**3**	**18**
other 'active' sport‡	8	5	2	2	0	**4**	**41**
N (base)	627	656	525	462	482	**2,752**	**6,703**

Source: General Household Survey 1990

Notes:
* 'No physical exercise' means that the person had not taken a walk of two miles or more in the past year, gone swimming, played bowls or soccer, or done any physical exercise listed on show cards (a list of 32 sports, of which the last is 'any other sport or physical activity')
† 'passive' sports comprise fishing, snooker and billiards, and darts
‡ 'active' sports comprise all other active sports, apart from those already listed (swimming, bowls, golf and keep fit)

Among the activities asked about, walking was the most popular, with three in five of the older men and two in five of the women having been for a walk of at least two miles in the past year. Swimming was the next most popular active pursuit, and for women 'keep fit'. (Fifteen per cent of the men and 11% of the women had been swimming; and 8% of the women had been to 'keep fit' sessions.) 'Passive' sport was also popular among the men, with one in six taking part in activities such as fishing, snooker and darts. Since taking part in a sporting activity at least once in the past year is not a good guide to how physically active people are, we show in **Table 3.5** the same activities for the past four weeks. The proportions are of course lower, but even so a half of the men and a third of the women had taken part in some sporting activity in the past month.

Table 3.5 Sporting activities in the past four weeks, by age group and gender, people aged 60 and over and 16–59, Great Britain, 1990

	60–64 years	65–69 years	70–74 years	75–79 years	80 yrs & over	60 yrs & over	16–59 years
	%	%	%	%	%	%	%
Men							
no physical exercise*	40	40	45	57	79	48	20
walk of 10+ miles	3	2	1	1	1	2	3
walk of 5–9 miles	14	14	11	7	4	11	13
walk of 2–5 miles	45	43	42	31	16	38	44
swimming	7	7	4	1	0	5	17
bowls	5	6	5	3	1	5	3
cycling	7	7	6	6	2	6	14
golf	6	5	4	3	1	4	11
keep fit	5	4	5	3	3	4	7
'passive' sport†	12	11	8	5	2	9	37
other 'active' sport‡	8	4	3	2	0	4	41
N (base)	582	572	419	273	245	**2,091**	**6,028**
Women							
no physical exercise*	48	56	65	75	88	65	34
walk of 10+ miles	1	1	1	0	0	1	1
walk of 5–9 miles	8	7	6	3	1	5	9
walk of 2–5 miles	41	36	28	20	9	28	40
swimming	8	7	2	2	0	4	20
bowls	3	3	2	1	0	2	1
cycling	7	3	2	1	0	3	8
golf	2	2	0	0	0	1	2
keep fit	9	8	6	3	2	6	20
'passive' sport†	2	1	1	1	0	1	10
other 'active' sport‡	3	2	2	1	0	2	19
N (base)	627	656	525	462	482	**2,752**	**6,703**

Source: General Household Survey 1990

Notes: see Table 3.4

People with limiting long-standing illnesses were, as one would expect, less likely to take part in sporting activities than others (**Table 3.6**); even so, in the past year 54% of the men and 33% of the women *had* participated.

Disabled older people (**Table 3.7**) were much less likely to go out for social activities (which could include leisure and perhaps sport), with four out of five – when asked whether they 'regularly go anywhere for training or social activities' – saying that they 'don't go anywhere'; 16% said they had visited a social club of some sort. (We do not have specific information about sport for disabled older people.)

Our figures certainly *appear* to suggest that women are less physically active than men. But this is not entirely confirmed by other surveys. For example the Allied Dunbar National Fitness Survey of 1990 found that for people aged 65–74 years in the previous four weeks *in*activity had been slightly more common among men than women. Forty-four per cent of the men and 40% of the women had been *in*active, i.e. had spent *no* occasions engaging in a 'mix of moderate and vigorous activity'; 23% of the men and 19% of the women had had '12 or more occasions of moderate activity' or of 'vigorous activity' (Allied Dunbar, 1992:p6). ('Virtually all vigorous activities were achieved through sport and recreation', though 'activities in and around the home made a significant contribution to moderate activity levels over the previous four weeks'; Allied Dunbar, 1992.) This finding supports the view that part of the reason why women participate less than men in physical *leisure* pursuits is that they are spending more time on physical domestic or caring activities.

The National Travel Survey also tells us about the way in which older people get out and about for recreational purposes. For example, the average mileage walked per person per year is an interesting indicator of the extent to which people get around actively outside the home (though it does not of course confine itself to leisure purposes).

For men, average walking distance per year increased sharply at age 65–69 (i.e. just post state pension age), from an 'under 60' average of 239 miles a year in 1989/91 to 283 miles a year (**Figure 3.5**). Thereafter it declined, gently at first, then rapidly after the age of 75. Women under the age of 60 walked a considerably higher average annual mileage than men, but in later life they walked less than men, and the difference between the sexes widened from 65 years upwards, being at its greatest for people in their late eighties when men walked in 1989/91 on average 100 miles more than women per annum (obviously related to women's greater chances of being disabled).

Table 3.6 Sporting activities in the past 12 months, by presence of limiting long-standing illness and gender, people aged 60 and over, Great Britain, 1990

	Limiting long-standing illness	Non-limiting long-standing illness	No long-standing illness	All aged 60 yrs & over
	%	%	%	%
Men				
walked 2 miles or more	41	69	69	**58**
did any physical exercise at all*	54	78	80	**69**
N (base)	854	394	830	**2,078**
Women				
walked 2 miles or more	26	55	56	**43**
did any physical exercise at all*	33	63	63	**50**
N (base)	1,168	526	1,037	**2,731**

Source: General Household Survey 1990.

Note: * For definition of 'physical exercise', see Table 3.4 above

Table 3.7 Disabled adults regularly going to places for training or social activities, by gender, disabled people aged 60 and over living in private households, 1985

	Men	Women	Men & women
	%	%	%
Doesn't go anywhere	81	77	**79**
Day centre	4	6	**5**
Adult training centre	0	0	**0**
Club for disabled	2	2	**2**
Other social club	15	17	**16**
Adult education	1	1	**1**
Other	1	2	**1**
N (weighted)	2,656	4,133	**6,789**
N (unweighted)	2,129	3,108	**5,237**

Source: Disability Survey 1985

Notes:
Proportions sum to more than 100% because some people attended more than one place regularly.
The OPCS Surveys of Disabled Adults in private households deliberately undersampled people aged 60 years and over. In calculating proportions, means etc. the sample numbers have been weighted to correct for this, other aspects of sample design and to adjust for certain kinds of non-response (see Martin et al, 1988, for further details). The unweighted sample numbers are also shown in order to indicate statistical reliability.

Figure 3.5 Average annual walking distance, by age group and gender, Great Britain

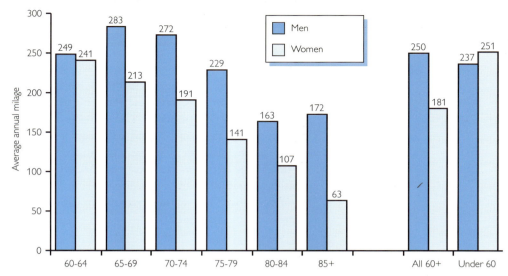

Source: National Travel Survey 1989–91, unpublished data, commissioned from Department of Transport, Statistics Division

The average number of miles people travel in the course of a year, by all means of transport, for leisure purposes also says something about the nature of these pursuits and the differences between people. **Figure 3.6** shows that in 1989/91 for all age groups until very late age people travelled further in a year for leisure than for any other purpose (excluding journeys under one mile), though if one combines commuting and business travel then for working age men these exceeded travel for leisure. As one would expect, travel for leisure declines gradually with age for both men and women, though until very late age it remains by far the most important purpose of journeys, with shopping and personal business coming a very poor second and third.

Figure 3.6 Average annual mileage travelled by a) men and b) women, excluding journeys under one mile, by journey purpose and by age group, Great Britain, 1989–91

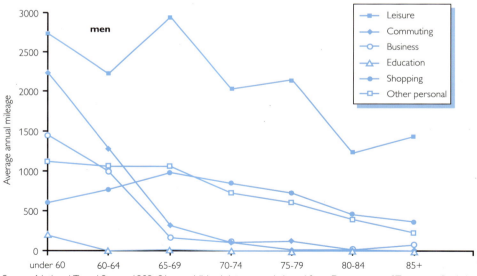

Source: National Travel Survey 1989–91, unpublished data, commissioned from Department of Transport, Statistics Division

Figure 3.6 cont. Average annual mileage travelled by a) men and b) women, excluding journeys under one mile, by journey purpose and by age group, Great Britain, 1989–91

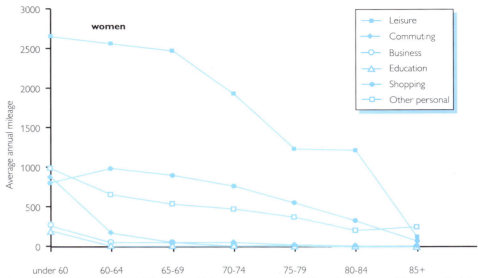

Source: National Travel Survey 1989–91, unpublished data, commissioned from Department of Transport, Statistics Division

For people in their early eighties in 1989/91, 70% of the travel miles of women and 59% of the travel miles of men were for leisure (defined for the purposes of this survey as all journeys not for the purpose of work/business, personal business/ medical, education or shopping). Even though a smaller proportion of the older men's total mileage was for leisure than that of older women, older men travelled more miles for leisure because their overall mileage was greater (except for those aged 60–64 where a higher proportion of the men's mileage was for work than for leisure, and for those aged 90 years and over where, however, sample numbers are far too small for analysis).

Travelling further afield: holidays

Our previous report showed that in 1988 a quarter of the older population of the United Kingdom were in households which had paid for a holiday in the past three months (Askham et al, 1992, **Table 7.4**). In the 1991 Family Expenditure Survey the figures were much the same overall (**Table 3.8**), though there was a slight increase in holidays for the younger old population and a slight drop for the older old.

Table 3.8 Holidays paid for in the past three months, by age group, people aged 60 and over, United Kingdom, 1991

	60–64 years	65–69 years	70–74 years	75–79 years	80 yrs & over	60 yrs & over
	%	%	%	%	%	%
Any holiday paid for	33	25	25	18	14	**24**
UK	19	15	16	14	11	**15**
Abroad	18	12	11	4	4	**11**
Package	19	14	13	7	7	**13**
Hotel	9	8	10	8	5	**8**
Self catering	9	5	4	5	2	**5**
N (base)	876	879	703	574	510	**3,542**

Source: Family Expenditure Survey 1991

Update of *Life After 60*, Table 7.4

Note: These figures refer to older people living in a household in which a holiday (or holidays) had been paid for in the past three months

Again the proportion declined with age, but even so 14% of those aged 80 and over were in households which had paid for a holiday. For younger elderly people, holidays in the UK only just exceeded visits abroad, but for the more elderly they predominated. Package holidays remained popular, especially for those in younger late life. Those in the lower income groups were less likely to have a paid holiday (**Table 3.9**); for example 10% of those in the lowest income quartile had one compared with 39% of those in the highest quartile; and only two per cent of the former group had paid for a holiday abroad.

Table 3.9 Holidays paid for in the past three months, by income quartile, people aged 60 and over, United Kingdom, 1991

	First (lowest)	Second	Third	Fourth (highest)	All aged 60 & over
	%	%	%	%	
Any holiday paid for	10	20	28	39	**24**
UK	8	15	18	21	**15**
Abroad	2	6	13	22	**11**
Package	5	11	16	20	**13**
Hotel	2	6	9	16	**8**
Self catering	3	5	6	8	**5**
N (base)	888	883	887	884	**3,542**

Source: Family Expenditure Survey 1991

Update of *Life After 60*, Table 7.5

Notes: see note to Table 3.8
Income is equivalent net household income, as used in Chapter 2

The International Passenger Survey of 1991 adds to the picture (**Table 3.10**) by showing that when people travelled abroad it was mainly to have a holiday rather than to visit friends or relatives; around five times the number of people went on holiday rather than to visit friends or relatives. However, when older people (65 years and over) travelled abroad they spent on average 38 days away if they were visiting friends or relatives (much longer than younger people going for the same purpose) and 14 days if they went for a holiday (slightly longer than younger people).

Table 3.10 People travelling abroad in 1991, by age group and purpose, United Kingdom, 1991

	Visit to friends or relatives	Average length of stay (days)	Holiday	Average length of stay (days)
	%		%	
Age group:				
0–15 years	12	27	12	12
16–24 years	17	24	15	13
25–34 years	20	18	19	12
35–44 years	14	18	18	11
45–54 years	15	18	18	12
55–64 years	12	22	11	12
65 years & over	10	38	7	14
N (base)	4,341		21,856	

Source: International Passenger Survey 1991, unpublished data, commissioned from the Department of National Heritage, Statistics Division

For disabled older people also the taking of holidays declines with age (**Table 3.11**). In 1985 just over half the younger elderly people had taken a holiday or break in the last year, whereas the proportions – for both men and women – dropped to a third for those aged 85 and over.

Table 3.11 Disabled adults taking a holiday or break in the past year, by age group, disabled adults living in private households, Great Britain, 1985

	Men			Women		
	%	N	N	%	N	N
		(weighted)	(unweighted)		(weighted)	(unweighted)
Age group:						
16–59 years	50	1,486	2,507	58	1,724	2,880
60–64 years	55	585	561	60	494	464
65–69 years	52	537	440	53	630	511
70–74 years	48	570	457	56	795	629
75–79 years	45	489	361	48	895	671
80–84 years	34	314	212	45	751	503
85 yrs & over	33	163	98	33	569	330

Source: Disability Survey 1985

Note: for information about weighted and unweighted samples see note to Table 3.7.

Disabled women kept up their holidays slightly longer than disabled men, with 45% of the women in their early eighties taking a holiday or break compared with 34% of the men in that age group. Their holidays/breaks were usually spent either in an ordinary holiday home or with friends or family (**Table 3.12**); though we have no information about whether they went abroad or stayed in the United Kingdom.

Table 3.12 Place of holiday or break taken by disabled adults in the past year, by gender, disabled people aged 60 and over, living in private households, Great Britain, 1985

	Men	Women	Men & women
	%	%	%
Ordinary holiday home	62	51	**55**
Family/friends	48	54	**52**
Hospital, nursing or convalescent home	4	5	**4**
Hostel or Local Authority home	2	3	**2**
Disabled organisation home	1	1	**1**
Private family	1	1	**1**
Other	1	1	**1**
N (weighted)	1,252	2,031	**3,283**
N (unweighted)	1,023	1,567	**2,590**

Source: Disability Survey 1985

Note: for information about weighted and unweighted samples see note to Table 3.7.

For those who had not had a holiday (**Figure 3.7**), the main reason given was either to do with their health or because they did not want one, rather than because they could not afford it (though a quarter did give finance as the reason, and **Table 3.9** discussed above shows that among the general population of older people, income does appear to affect how often holidays are taken).

Figure 3.7 Reasons for disabled adults not taking a holiday, by gender, disabled people aged 60 and over, living in private households, Great Britain, 1985

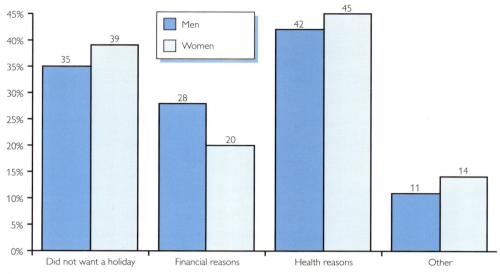

Source: Disability Survey 1985

Getting Around the Home

Some key facts*

- 80% of people aged 65 and over had no difficulty with any *personal* care task, but one person in ten found at least one *personal* care task very difficult or impossible

- 68% of people aged 65 and over had no difficulty with any *domestic* task, but one person in five found at least one *domestic* task very difficult or impossible. A quarter of all women found at least one *domestic* task very difficult or impossible, the most difficult task being cleaning windows

- 69% of people aged 65 and over had no difficulty with any *locomotive* task, but 13% found at least one *locomotive* task very difficult or impossible. The hardest task was getting up and down stairs

- difficulty with tasks (*personal, domestic or locomotive*) varied by gender, living arrangements and age:

    17% of men and 27% of women found at least one task very difficult or impossible (two-thirds of men but only just over half of women had no difficulty with any task)

    28% of people who lived alone found at least one task very difficult or impossible (only half had no difficulty with any task); for those who lived with a spouse only 16% found at least one task very difficult or impossible, and two-thirds had no difficulty with any task

    over half of men aged 85 and over, and two-thirds of the women found at least one task very difficult or impossible

- one-third of people aged 65 and over who needed help with domestic, locomotive or self-care tasks usually received help from a spouse and two-fifths from a son or daughter; a further 14% had help from some other relative

- 23% of men and 31% of women who found at least one task very difficult or impossible had a Local Authority home help

- while four out of five people over the age of 60 lived in a house the proportion dropped to two-thirds of those aged 85–89, and one in ten of the latter lived in a flat not at street level and without a lift. The older age groups were also least likely to have access to central heating, a microwave, a washing machine or a car

- relatively few disabled people over the age of 60 had special gadgets in 1985 (only 10% of men and one in five women) but half the women and one-third of men had special furniture and nearly a quarter of men and 30% of women had adaptations (such as hand-rails)

---

*All figures relate to Great Britain and to 1991 unless otherwise stated, and exclude people living in institutions

Retaining the ability to get around one's home is very important for independence in later life. It contributes much to the quality of life in old age, affecting both physical and psychological well-being. The extent to which older people may experience problems in looking after themselves and their homes and moving around their homes is the subject of this Chapter. We look at problems stemming from their own frailties, and also examine how the conditions in which they live – physical aspects of their homes, whether they live alone or with others, and the help they receive from family, friends and formal services – may affect everyday life within the home.

The analysis draws in particular on the special section of the 1991 General Household Survey that asked those aged 65 years and over about their ability to undertake a wide range of tasks important for independent living. We look especially at tasks involving getting around and using facilities in the home: personal care tasks such as washing and dressing; mobility around the home (including getting up and down stairs or in and out of bed); and looking after the home (washing-up, doing the laundry and vacuum cleaning for example). A later chapter investigates problems related to movement outside the home, for example doing the shopping.

We start with a brief consideration of the factors which influence independence in the home. This is followed first by some analysis of the physical conditions in which older people live, then by an analysis of older people's abilities to undertake everyday activities within the home. We finish with a discussion of help received from people and special equipment.

Independence at home

The ability to get around the home is affected by one's own health and by the state of the home itself. Moving about the home, performing every day tasks of personal care and housework can become difficult in later life due to physical or mental frailty. The impact of increasing frailty may depend crucially on the physical state of the home. Problems can be exacerbated or mitigated by the layout of the home, or alleviated by practical aids and adaptations. If the need to go up and downstairs throughout the day can be avoided, the consequences of impairments may be considerably less than if, for example, the only toilet is upstairs. The arrangement of older people's own homes is our main concern, but their ability to negotiate the homes of friends and relatives is also important. If they are unable to cope with steps and stairs, the home of a friend or relative in a flat above ground floor level may be inaccessible.

How difficult or easy it is for an older person to move about the home also depends on whether help is near at hand from other members of the household. The consequences of not being able to get around the home are likely to be more serious for older people who live alone than for those who live with others. Help given by family members, friends and neighbours as well as formal services are all important in maintaining independence within the home.

The home itself

Four out of five elderly people over the age of 60 lived in a whole house in 1991 (**Table 4.1**).

Table 4.1 Type of accommodation, by gender, people aged 60 and over, Great Britain, 1991

	Men	Women	Men & women
	%	%	%
Whole house	84	78	**81**
Purpose-built flat:			
with lift or at street level	6	10	**9**
without lift and not at street level	6	8	**7**
House conversion/part of house:			
with lift or at street level	2	2	**2**
without lift and not at street level	1	1	**1**
Other	1	1	**1**
N (base)	2,163	2,853	**5,016**

Source: General Household Survey 1991

This type of housing can present problems as physical mobility declines and stairs become difficult to negotiate. Many of these houses are likely to be without a downstairs toilet and the older person may thus have to go up and down the stairs throughout the day in order to use the toilet. If stairs cannot be negotiated then the older person may opt to sleep downstairs even though this means there is not a toilet within easy reach. Neither is satisfactory. **Table 4.1** also shows that eight per cent of people aged 60 and over lived in a purpose built flat or converted house without a lift on a floor that was not at street level (nearly all of them lived *above* street level). Most of those not living at street level lived on the first floor but one in five lived on the second floor or above (**Table 4.2**). Again there may be problems here for people who are less mobile. There is a steady decline in the proportions living in a whole house by age (87% of people aged 60–64 lived in a whole house, compared with only 69% of people aged 85–89), which is almost wholly compensated for by a rise in the proportions living in a flat with a lift or at street level (from five per cent of people aged 60–64 to 18% of people aged 85–89). There was, however, a small rise in the proportions of people living in a flat without a lift and not at street level, from seven per cent of people aged 60–64 to 11% of people aged 85–89 (General Household Survey 1991, own analysis, table not presented here).

Table 4.2 Floor level of those living in a flat/house conversion, not at street level, and without a lift, by gender, people aged 60 and over, Great Britain, 1991

	Men	Women	Men & women
	%	%	%
Basement	1	1	**1**
First floor	72	78	**76**
Second floor	24	17	**19**
Third floor	3	3	**3**
Fourth floor	0	0	**0**
N (base)	144	237	**380**

Source: General Household Survey 1991

By 1985, virtually all people aged 60 and over lived in households with an inside toilet and 99% lived in homes with a fixed bath or shower connected to a hot water supply (**Table 4.3**). Nonetheless, six per cent of those aged 90 and over, and three per cent of those aged between 75 and 89 years did not possess a bath.

Table 4.3 Possession of selected household amenities, 1980, 1985, 1991, by age group, people aged 60 and over, Great Britain

	60–64 years	65–69 years	70–74 years	75–79 years	80–84 years	85–89 years	90yrs & over	60 yrs & over
	%	%	%	%	%	%	%	%
1980								
central heating	51	50	48	46	39	44	(51)	**48**
car	58	47	38	25	19	21	(27)	**42**
bath	98	98	95	96	94	90	(90)	**96**
flush toilet	99	99	99	98	98	97	(98)	**99**
N (base)	1,675	1,653	1,245	878	451	208	(49)	**6,159**
1985								
central heating	66	67	64	62	62	59	61	**64**
car	66	56	41	33	25	23	23	**48**
bath	99	99	99	97	97	97	94	**99**
flush toilet	100	100	100	100	100	100	100	**100**
N (base)	1,509	1,137	1,063	818	413	198	62	**5,200**
1991								
central heating	85	81	78	75	72	71	71	**79**
car	72	62	51	39	31	23	25	**53**
N (base)	1,218	1,254	941	818	489	211	83	**5,014**

Source: General Household Survey 1980, 1985, 1991

Notes: 'bath' = fixed bath or fixed shower with hot water supply
'flush toilet' = flush toilet inside accommodation
In 1991, the questions on bath and flush toilet were not asked (see text).
Percentages in brackets are based on small numbers and should be used with caution.

Although questions on a flush toilet and bath were not asked in the 1991 General Household Survey, on the assumption that almost everyone would have both, the 1991 Census of Population revealed that a small minority (1.4%) of people of pensionable age lacked or shared with another household a bath/shower and/or inside toilet (see Appendix A, **Table A.9**). Most disturbing is the fact that 3.4% of people aged 85 and over – some 22,000 people – came into this category. Lack of such amenities amongst some of our oldest members of society, or the need to share them with another household, is obviously detrimental to older people's general well-being and is likely to intensify any problems they have in moving around.

During the 1980s there was a considerable rise in the proportion of older people living in households with central heating. Whereas only half of people aged 60 and over in 1980, and two thirds in 1985, had central heating, by 1991 four out of five were living in households with some form of central heating (**Table 4.3**). The very old were less likely to have central heating than the younger elderly. Three in ten people aged 85 and over did not have central heating in 1991. Not only does central heating generally provide more adequate and often cheaper heating, it usually requires less physical strength to operate compared with, for example, solid fuel fires or electric heaters that may have to be moved from one room to another; although the fact that people have central heating does not, of course, necessarily mean that they will use it.

General health General health has an important effect on how well a person can manage at home. In 1991 some two-fifths of people aged 60 years and over reported having a long-standing illness, disability or infirmity that limited their activities (see

Appendix A, **Table A.14**). For men, this proportion was relatively stable across age groups although, as would be expected, some increase with age is apparent. Forty per cent of men aged 60–64 years reported a limiting long-standing illness compared with nearly a half of those aged 80 years and over. There was a steadier and sharper increase in the proportion of women reporting a long-standing illness that limited their activities, from 29% of those aged 60–64 to 54% of women aged 80 years or more. Thus within the population of older people, men seem more likely than women to suffer from a limiting long-standing illness below the age of 75 years whereas at older ages the situation is reversed. Some of this difference may be due to differences in expectations, for example, about what it is 'normal' to be able to do at certain ages.

To gain a clearer understanding of older people's abilities it is possible to look at how well they say they manage specific tasks related to looking after themselves and moving around the home. However, even here perceptions of how easy it is to carry out certain activities cannot provide entirely 'objective' indicators.

Personal care   **Table 4.4** shows the levels of difficulty people aged 65 and over had in 1991 with selected personal care tasks.

Table 4.4 Levels of difficulty with selected personal care tasks, by age group and gender, people aged 65 and over, Great Britain, 1991

Men	65–69 years	70–74 years	75–79 years	80–84 years	85–89 years	90 yrs & over	65 yrs & over
	%	%	%	%	%	%	%
Washing self all over							
not difficult	95	94	88	85	54	(75)	**90**
quite difficult	3	2	5	7	22	(8)	**5**
very difficult	2	2	3	3	11	(13)	**3**
impossible	1	2	3	4	13	(4)	**2**
Dressing/undressing							
not difficult	93	93	89	83	73	(79)	**90**
quite difficult	5	3	6	10	10	(13)	**5**
very difficult	1	2	4	4	11	(0)	**3**
impossible	1	2	1	3	6	(8)	**2**
Feeding self							
not difficult	98	98	97	93	79	(96)	**97**
quite difficult	1	0	2	5	14	(4)	**2**
very difficult	0	0	1	2	5	(0)	**1**
impossible	0	1	0	1	2	(0)	**1**
Using toilet							
not difficult	99	98	95	96	83	(92)	**97**
quite difficult	1	1	3	3	11	(4)	**2**
very difficult	0	1	1	0	3	(4)	**1**
impossible	0	0	1	1	3	(0)	**1**
Preparing a hot meal							
not difficult	95	93	87	77	57	(75)	**89**
quite difficult	3	3	6	9	8	(0)	**4**
very difficult	2	1	2	5	8	(13)	**2**
impossible	1	3	6	9	27	(13)	**5**
No difficulty with any personal care task	90	88	82	71	46	(58)	**83**
At least one personal care task							
very difficult or impossible	5	7	10	16	43	(29)	**10**
N (base)	541	408	330	178	63	(24)	**1,544**

Source: General Household Survey 1991

Table 4.4 cont. Levels of difficulty with selected personal care tasks, by age group and gender, people aged 65 and over, Great Britain, 1991

Women	65–69 years	70–74 years	75–79 years	80–84 years	85–89 years	90 yrs & over	65 yrs & over
	%	%	%	%	%	%	%
Washing self all over							
not difficult	94	92	84	80	69	46	**87**
quite difficult	3	4	9	12	14	19	**7**
very difficult	2	3	4	6	8	14	**4**
impossible	1	2	3	2	8	21	**3**
Dressing/undressing							
not difficult	94	92	85	80	74	58	**87**
quite difficult	4	5	11	15	13	16	**8**
very difficult	1	2	3	4	8	7	**3**
impossible	1	2	1	1	6	19	**2**
Feeding self							
not difficult	99	98	95	94	88	79	**96**
quite difficult	1	1	4	5	7	11	**3**
very difficult	0	1	1	0	3	2	**1**
impossible	0	0	0	0	1	9	**1**
Using toilet							
not difficult	99	98	96	94	91	77	**96**
quite difficult	1	1	2	5	5	11	**2**
very difficult	0	0	0	1	2	4	**0**
impossible	0	1	1	0	2	9	**1**
Preparing a hot meal							
not difficult	95	94	87	83	63	46	**88**
quite difficult	2	2	7	7	17	12	**5**
very difficult	2	2	2	4	8	14	**3**
impossible	1	2	4	6	13	28	**4**
No difficulty with any personal care task	90	87	76	68	53	32	**79**
At least one personal care task very difficult or impossible	5	7	11	16	28	53	**11**
N (base)	676	518	474	302	144	57	**2,171**

Source: General Household Survey 1991

The majority of elderly people reported no problems at all with many of the tasks. Indeed, 83% of men aged 65 and over and 79% of women of that age had no difficulty with any of the personal care tasks listed. Least difficulty was experienced with feeding and using the toilet. Over 95% of men and women had no difficulty feeding themselves and the same percentages could use the toilet without difficulty. Preparing a hot meal presented some difficulty for the highest proportions of older people: 12% of women and 11% of men found preparing a hot meal at least quite difficult.

The ability to undertake these tasks shows a steady decline with increasing age. The steepest decline is seen in the ability to wash all over and to prepare a hot meal. Close to 95% of men and women aged 65 to 69 years found no difficulty with these tasks in 1991. Within the age group 85–89 years, however, only 69% of women experienced no difficulties washing themselves all over and only 63% could prepare a hot meal without some difficulty. For men the corresponding proportions were lower still: 54% and 57% respectively.

Looking at tasks which people found impossible, preparing a hot meal presented the biggest challenge for both men and women aged 85–89 years. At 27%, the proportion of men in this age group who could not prepare a hot meal was roughly twice that for women. (Preparing food, however, is often regarded as a gender-specific task, and the high proportions of men finding it impossible to prepare a hot meal at very old ages might well reflect this, rather than true ability.)

Men aged 90 years and over appeared to have fewer difficulties than those aged 85–89 years. However, sample sizes for men aged at least 90 are too small to draw firm conclusions, and there is no corresponding finding amongst women. Higher proportions of women aged 90 and over found each task impossible than younger women, although again sample sizes are very small.

The ability to undertake personal care tasks is analysed according to living arrangements in **Table 4.5**. Elderly people living with others, not a spouse, had considerably more problems than those in other categories, although this is not surprising since those living with someone other than their spouse often do so *because* they need help. Elderly people living with others, not a spouse, also tend to be older than people living in other types of household (the mean age of people aged 60 and over living with others, not a spouse, was 73.7 years compared with 70.7 years for people in other living arrangements) and older people tend to be in poorer health and more likely to be suffering from a limiting long-standing illness (see **Tables A.13 and A.14** in Appendix A). Their problems were particularly noticeable for washing themselves all over and preparing a hot meal where only 77% and 72% respectively had no difficulty. Nearly a quarter of elderly people living with someone other than their spouse found at least one personal care task very difficult or impossible. Nonetheless, 64% had no difficulty with any of these tasks.

Table 4.5 Levels of difficulty with selected personal care tasks, by living arrangement, people aged 65 and over, Great Britain, 1991

	Lives alone	With spouse	With spouse and others	With others not spouse
	%	%	%	%
Washing self all over				
not difficult	86	91	91	77
quite difficult	8	4	5	8
very difficult	4	2	2	6
impossible	1	3	2	8
Dressing/undressing				
not difficult	88	91	90	78
quite difficult	8	5	6	13
very difficult	3	2	3	4
impossible	1	2	2	5
Feeding self				
not difficult	97	97	97	90
quite difficult	3	2	1	6
very difficult	0	1	0	2
impossible	0	1	1	2
Using toilet				
not difficult	97	97	99	92
quite difficult	3	2	1	4
very difficult	0	1	0	1
impossible	0	1	0	2
Preparing a hot meal				
not difficult	89	91	91	72
quite difficult	5	4	4	9
very difficult	3	2	2	7
impossible	3	4	3	13
No difficulty with any personal care task	80	86	81	64
At least one personal care task very difficult or impossible	10	8	10	24
N (base)	1,400	1,721	221	373

Source: General Household Survey 1991

It can also be seen from **Table 4.5** that some people who lived alone experienced difficulties that must present problems. Six per cent found it very difficult or impossible to prepare a hot meal, five per cent to wash all over and four per cent to dress and undress. For such fundamental tasks it must be a matter of concern that 10% found at least one personal care task very difficult or impossible.

Domestic tasks The special section on elderly people in the 1991 General Household Survey also asked about an extensive list of domestic tasks that are entailed in living in one's own home. Four seem particularly pertinent to 'looking after the home': washing and drying dishes; using a vacuum cleaner; cleaning inside windows; and doing small amounts of washing by hand. In general, the proportions having difficulty with all these tasks increased with age (**Table 4.6**).

Table 4.6 Levels of difficulty with selected domestic tasks, by age and gender, people aged 65 and over, Great Britain, 1991

Men	65–69 years	70–74 years	75–79 years	80–84 years	85–89 years	90 yrs & over	65 yrs & over
	%	%	%	%	%	%	%
Washing and drying dishes							
not difficult	97	96	93	91	72	(88)	**94**
quite difficult	2	1	2	4	13	(4)	**3**
very difficult	1	1	1	2	3	(0)	**1**
impossible	1	2	3	3	13	(8)	**2**
Using a vacuum cleaner							
not difficult	92	90	85	75	59	(54)	**86**
quite difficult	5	4	7	11	5	(25)	**6**
very difficult	2	2	2	7	8	(8)	**3**
impossible	2	3	6	8	28	(13)	**5**
Cleaning inside windows							
not difficult	89	84	78	69	38	(46)	**80**
quite difficult	5	8	8	11	19	(17)	**8**
very difficult	3	3	5	5	11	(17)	**4**
impossible	2	5	9	14	33	(21)	**7**
Doing small amounts of laundry by hand							
not difficult	93	92	86	77	58	(63)	**87**
quite difficult	3	3	4	8	10	(17)	**4**
very difficult	2	2	2	6	5	(8)	**3**
impossible	2	3	8	9	27	(13)	**5**
No difficulty with any domestic task	86	84	76	65	32	(38)	**78**
At least one domestic task very difficult or impossible	7	8	16	22	47	(38)	**13**
N (base)	550	416	336	183	64	(24)	**1,573**

Source: General Household Survey 1991

Table 4.6 cont. Levels of difficulty with selected domestic tasks, by age and gender, people aged 65 and over, Great Britain, 1991

Women	65–69 years	70–74 years	75–79 years	80–84 years	85–89 years	90 yrs & over	65 yrs & over
	%	%	%	%	%	%	%
Washing and drying dishes							
not difficult	96	96	92	92	84	65	**93**
quite difficult	2	2	4	4	9	13	**3**
very difficult	1	1	2	2	1	5	**1**
impossible	1	1	2	2	7	16	**2**
Using a vacuum cleaner							
not difficult	87	81	73	59	47	27	**75**
quite difficult	7	10	12	17	20	9	**11**
very difficult	2	3	8	11	14	16	**6**
impossible	3	6	8	14	19	47	**9**
Cleaning inside windows							
not difficult	82	72	60	45	31	16	**65**
quite difficult	9	14	15	17	17	13	**13**
very difficult	4	6	9	11	23	13	**8**
impossible	5	8	16	28	29	58	**14**
Doing small amounts of laundry by hand							
not difficult	91	89	83	79	68	40	**85**
quite difficult	4	5	7	10	12	9	**6**
very difficult	2	3	5	4	6	15	**4**
impossible	2	3	6	7	14	36	**6**
No difficulty with any domestic task	80	69	58	40	28	15	**62**
At least one domestic task very difficult or impossible	10	17	27	40	53	76	**24**
N (base)	689	522	477	303	146	55	**2,192**

Source: General Household Survey 1991

Particularly striking are the declining proportions who had no difficulty with any domestic task and the rise in those who found at least one domestic task very difficult or impossible (three-quarters of women aged 90 or more were in this position). Using a vacuum cleaner posed no difficulties for 87% of women and 92% of men aged 65–69 but this fell to 27% of women and 54% of men aged 90 and over. Difficulty was most frequently experienced with cleaning inside windows. Even in the youngest age group, five per cent of women and two per cent of men could not clean the inside of their windows. Over the age of 90, more than a half of women and one in five men found it impossible. Although numbers of people aged 90 and over are again small it is interesting that for washing and drying dishes and for cleaning inside windows such men had fewer problems than those aged 85–89 years.

Older people living with others, not a spouse, were less able to perform these domestic tasks than those in other living arrangements (**Table 4.7**), just as they tended to have more problems with personal care tasks. Those living alone also had problems: two per cent found it very difficult or impossible to wash and dry dishes; nine per cent to do small amounts of washing by hand; 14% to use a vacuum cleaner; and 22% to clean inside their windows.

Table 4.7 Levels of difficulty with selected domestic tasks, by living arrangement, people aged 65 and over, Great Britain, 1991

	Lives alone	With spouse only	With spouse and others	With others not spouse
	%	%	%	%
Washing and drying dishes				
not difficult	95	95	95	82
quite difficult	4	2	2	7
very difficult	1	1	0	3
impossible	1	2	3	8
Using a vacuum cleaner				
not difficult	75	85	84	65
quite difficult	11	7	6	10
very difficult	6	3	6	8
impossible	8	5	4	17
Cleaning inside windows				
not difficult	64	80	78	54
quite difficult	14	8	10	13
very difficult	9	4	5	8
impossible	13	8	6	25
Doing small amounts of laundry by hand				
not difficult	86	89	87	70
quite difficult	6	4	4	10
very difficult	4	3	4	6
impossible	5	4	5	14
No difficulty with any domestic task	61	77	76	51
At least one domestic task very difficult or impossible	23	13	15	35
N (base)	1,414	1,749	223	379

Source: General Household Survey 1991

Getting around the home

Looking at the difficulties elderly people have with getting up and down stairs, in and out of bed and in and out of a chair, stairs present the greatest problems. Nine per cent of men, and 15% of women aged 65 and over found it very difficult or impossible in 1991 to get up and down stairs (**Table 4.8**).

Table 4.8 Levels of difficulty with selected locomotive tasks, by age and gender, people aged 65 and over, Great Britain, 1991

Men	65–69 years	70–74 years	75–79 years	80–84 years	85–89 years	90 yrs & over	65 yrs & over
	%	%	%	%	%	%	%
Getting up and down stairs							
not difficult	85	80	71	67	43	(50)	**76**
quite difficult	9	14	18	21	24	(21)	**14**
very difficult	4	4	7	8	17	(25)	**6**
impossible	1	2	4	4	16	(4)	**3**
Getting in and out of bed							
not difficult	94	95	92	89	68	(83)	**92**
quite difficult	4	3	7	7	19	(8)	**5**
very difficult	1	1	1	2	6	(8)	**2**
impossible	1	1	1	2	6	(0)	**1**
Getting in and out of chair							
not difficult	96	94	91	87	65	(79)	**92**
quite difficult	3	5	8	10	25	(13)	**6**
very difficult	0	0	1	2	6	(8)	**1**
impossible	0	0	1	2	3	(0)	**1**
					43 {		
No difficulty with any locomotive task	84	78	69	67	40	(50)	**75**
At least one locomotive task very difficult							
or impossible	6	7	12	12	35 }	(29)	**10**
						32	
N (base)	541	408	330	178	63	(24)	**1,544**

Source: General Household Survey 1991

Table 4.8 Levels of difficulty with selected locomotive tasks, by age and gender, people aged 65 and over, Great Britain, 1991

Women	65–69 years	70–74 years	75–79 years	80–84 years	85–89 years	90 yrs & over	65 yrs & over
	%	%	%	%	%	%	%
Getting up and down stairs							
not difficult	80	71	60	51	38	25	**65**
quite difficult	14	18	24	24	33	30	**20**
very difficult	4	6	9	14	13	18	**8**
impossible	2	4	7	10	16	28	**7**
Getting in and out of bed							
not difficult	95	92	88	83	76	63	**89**
quite difficult	3	6	9	12	16	23	**8**
very difficult	1	1	3	4	6	9	**2**
impossible	1	1	1	0	2	5	**1**
Getting in and out of chair							
not difficult	94	91	84	83	72	56	**87**
quite difficult	5	7	13	14	22	32	**10**
very difficult	1	1	2	2	6	9	**2**
impossible	1	1	1	1	1	4	**1**
					32 {		
No difficulty with any locomotive task	79	70	58	51	35	25	**64**
At least one locomotive task very difficult							
or impossible	6	11	17	25	30 }	46	**15**
						35	
N (base)	676	518	474	302	144	57	**2,171**

Source: General Household Survey 1991

Women had more difficulties, especially with getting up and down stairs. The percentages who did not find stairs difficult dropped from 80% of women and 85% of men aged 65–69 to 38% of women and 43% of men aged 85–89 years. In the age group 65–69 years, the same proportion (six per cent) of men and women found at least one of these locomotive tasks very difficult or impossible. At older ages women generally became more likely than men to find one or more tasks very difficult or impossible. Among those aged 80–84 years, women were twice as likely as men to be in this position. The decline with age in the percentages having no difficulty with any locomotive tasks is steeper for men than for women. Seventy-nine per cent of women aged 65–69 years had no difficulty compared with a third of women aged 85 or more. The corresponding fall for men was from 84% to 43%.

Table 4.9 shows the already familiar pattern that elderly people who lived with others (not a spouse) were less able to do all three of these everyday activities.

Table 4.9 Levels of difficulty with selected locomotive tasks, by living arrangement, people aged 65 and over, Great Britain, 1991

	Lives alone	With spouse only	With spouse and others	With others not spouse
	%	%	%	%
Getting up and down stairs				
not difficult	64	76	78	58
quite difficult	20	15	16	23
very difficult	9	5	4	11
impossible	6	4	2	9
Getting in and out of bed				
not difficult	89	93	94	83
quite difficult	8	5	4	11
very difficult	2	1	2	4
impossible	0	2	0	2
Getting in and out of chair				
not difficult	88	92	93	80
quite difficult	11	6	6	15
very difficult	1	1	1	4
impossible	0	1	0	1
No difficulty with any locomotive task	63	75	76	56
At least one locomotive task				
very difficult or impossible	16	9	7	20
N (base)	1,400	1,721	221	373

Source: General Household Survey 1991

Substantial proportions of them found it very difficult or impossible to do specific tasks: 20% to get up and down stairs; six per cent to get in and out of bed; and five per cent to get in and out of a chair. One in five found at least one of these tasks very difficult or impossible. Again those living alone also experienced problems, with 15% of them finding that negotiating stairs was very difficult or impossible.

Table 4.10, a summary table, demonstrates clearly the increasing difficulty which older age groups experience with personal, domestic and locomotive tasks.

Table 4.10 Summary table: difficulties with personal, domestic and locomotive tasks, by age group and gender, people aged 65 and over, Great Britain, 1991

	65–69 years	70–74 years	75–79 years	80–84 years	85–89 years	90yrs & over	65 yrs & over
	%	%	%	%	%	%	%
Men							
No difficulty with any personal care task	90	88	82	71	46	(58)	**83**
No difficulty with any domestic task	86	84	76	65	32	(38)	**78**
No difficulty with any locomotive task	84	78	69	67	40	(50)	**65**
No difficulty with any task	76	70	62	52	25	(28)	**66**
						26	
At least one personal care task very difficult or impossible	5	7	10	16	43	(29)	**10**
At least one domestic task very difficult or impossible	7	8	16	22	47	(38)	**13**
At least one locomotive task very difficult or impossible	6	7	12	12	35	(29)	**10**
At least one task very difficult or impossible	10	14	20	26	53	(52)	**17**
						53	
N (base)	541	408	330	178	63	(24)	**1,544**
Women							
No difficulty with any personal care task	90	87	76	68	53	32	**79**
No difficulty with any domestic task	80	69	58	40	28	15	**62**
No difficulty with any locomotive task	79	70	58	51	35	25	**64**
No difficulty with any task	70	60	48	32	18	9	**53**
						16	
At least one personal care task very difficult or impossible	5	7	11	16	28	53	**11**
At least one domestic task very difficult or impossible	10	17	27	40	53	76	**24**
At least one locomotive task very difficult or impossible	6	11	17	25	30	46	**15**
At least one task very difficult or impossible	12	19	30	44	61	76	**27**
						65	
N (base)	676	518	474	302	144	57	**2,171**

Source: General Household Survey 1991

Amongst those aged 85 and over, more than a half of men and 65% of women found at least one personal care, domestic or locomotive task very difficult or impossible, compared with 10% and 12% respectively of those aged 65 to 69 years. The corresponding proportion having no difficulty with any task falls from three-quarters of men and 70% of women to a quarter and 16% respectively.

Figures 4.1 and **4.2** show clearly the gender differentials in difficulties with tasks.

Figure 4.1 Summary chart: proportions having no difficulty with any task, by age group and gender, people aged 65 and over, 1991

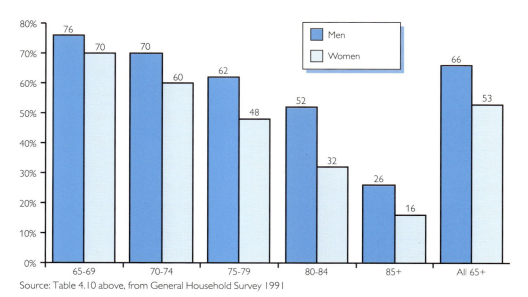

Source: Table 4.10 above, from General Household Survey 1991

Larger proportions of men in all age-groups over 65 had no difficulty with any task than women, and the gender differentials widen with increasing age. Conversely, smaller proportions of men in all age groups over 65 found at least one task very difficult or impossible, and again the gender differentials widen with age. At age 65–69, around one in ten of both men and women found at least one task very difficult or impossible, but by age 80–84 a quarter of men, but over two fifths of women, found at least one task very difficult or impossible.

Figure 4.2 Summary chart: proportions finding at least one task very difficult or impossible, by age group and gender, people aged 65 and over, 1991

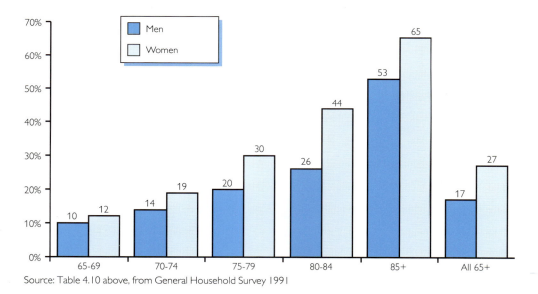

Source: Table 4.10 above, from General Household Survey 1991

Table 4.11 summarises the greater problems experienced by elderly people who live with people other than their spouse and also some of the problems faced by those who live alone. Nearly two-fifths of people aged 65 and over who lived with others but not with a spouse found at least one task very difficult or impossible. Nearly 30% of those who lived alone were in the same position. More than a half of those living with others and just under a half of those living alone faced *some* difficulty with at least one task.

Table 4.11 Summary table: difficulties with personal, domestic and locomotive tasks, by living arrangement, people aged 65 and over, Great Britain, 1991

	Lives alone	With spouse	With spouse and others	With others not spouse
	%	%	%	%
No difficulty with any personal care task	80	86	81	64
No difficulty with any domestic task	61	77	76	51
No difficulty with any locomotive task	63	75	76	56
No difficulty with any task	51	67	64	44
At least one personal care task very difficult or impossible	10	8	10	24
At least one domestic task very difficult or impossible	23	13	15	35
At least one locomotive task very difficult or impossible	16	9	7	20
At least one task very difficult or impossible	28	16	18	38
N (base)	1,400	1,721	221	373

Source: General Household Survey 1991

Help from other people

It is well known from existing studies that the main source of help given to older people who need help with personal, locomotive and domestic tasks is relatives – usually a spouse or child.

Figure 4.3 Sources of help for elderly people with domestic and locomotive/self care tasks, people aged 65 and over, Great Britain, 1991

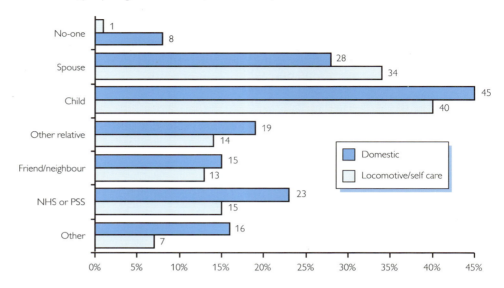

Source: Goddard and Savage, 1994: 29, 35 (data from General Household Survey, 1991)

Notes:
- 'NHS or PSS' = formal help from National Health Service or Personal Social Service professionals.
- 'Domestic' tasks = preparing meal, making cup of tea, doing washing up, using vacuum cleaner, cleaning inside windows, doing laundry, doing household shopping, dealing with personal affairs
- 'Locomotive/self care' tasks = walking down road, getting up and down stairs, getting in and out of bed, getting in and out of chair, washing all over, dressing, feeding self, using toilet on own

A third of people aged 65 years and over in 1991 who said they needed help with locomotive or self-care tasks (these include 'getting around outside the home' tasks – see notes to **Figure 4.3**) usually received help from a spouse. Two-fifths received help from a son or daughter. Fourteen per cent received help from some other relative. Thirteen per cent received help from a friend or neighbour, 15% from the NHS or their Local Authority and seven per cent received some other form of help. Eight per cent of all those aged 65 years and over who needed help with locomotive or self-care tasks did not usually receive help from anyone. More elderly people received help from formal services to assist with the domestic tasks involved in running a home than for locomotive or self-care tasks, although again most help came from family members (for further analysis and tabulations by household type, see Goddard and Savage, 1994).

In most cases formal help came from a Local Authority home help but in some cases it was from a private home help. (Very few had both Local Authority and private home helps.) **Table 4.12** shows that for most of the domestic tasks which elderly people found difficult, the proportion with either a Local Authority or private home help increased with the degree of difficulty experienced. However only 23% of men who found at least one personal, domestic or locomotive task very difficult or impossible, had a Local Authority home help and just eight per cent had a private home help. The comparable figures for women were 31% and 10%.

Table 4.12 Proportions of elderly people with Local Authority (LA) and private home helps, by degree of difficulty with selected domestic tasks, and by gender, people aged 65 and over, Great Britain, 1991

	Men			Women		
	LA home help	private home help	N (base)	LA home help	private home help	N (base)
	%	%		%	%	
Washing and drying dishes						
not difficult	5	4	1,475	9	5	2,034
quite difficult	(20)	(8)	(40)	41	6	71
very difficult	(11)	(6)	(18)	(32)	(13)	(31)
impossible	(17)	(6)	(35)	(36)	(11)	(45)
Using a vacuum cleaner						
not difficult	3	4	1,350	4	3	1,634
quite difficult	18	9	96	19	11	234
very difficult	(30)	(15)	(46)	34	11	131
impossible	24	3	76	46	13	182
Cleaning inside windows						
not difficult	3	3	1,260	2	3	1,416
quite difficult	10	8	126	14	6	286
very difficult	26	14	66	26	13	170
impossible	27	5	116	39	10	309
No difficulty with any personal, domestic or locomotive task	2	3	1,041	1	3	1,165
At least one personal, domestic or locomotive task very difficult or impossible	23	8	270	31	10	577

Source: General Household Survey 1991

Turning to specific tasks, of women who found it impossible to wash or dry dishes, 36% had a Local Authority home help in 1991 and 11% had a private one; of those who found it impossible to use a vacuum cleaner, 46% had a Local Authority home help and 13% a private one; and for cleaning inside and outside windows the figures were 39% and 10% respectively. Women were more likely than men to have a Local Authority or private home help. This probably reflects the facts that there are more women in older age groups, and thus they are more likely to live on their own and suffer from more severe disabilities.

When we standardise for age (**Table 4.13**), we find that larger proportions of women finding at least one task very difficult or impossible had a Local Authority home help. There is a relatively smooth increase in help received from formal sources with age; 16% of women aged 65–69 had a Local Authority home help and five per cent a private one, whereas for those aged 85–89 the figures were 44% and 17% respectively. For men the rise was from 11% and eight per cent to 35% and 12%. Again, we find some unexplained differences for people aged 90 and over when compared with people aged 85–89, but small sample numbers mean that it is impossible to draw conclusions. **Table 4.13** demonstrates clearly the preponderance of Local Authority help compared with that from private sources.

Table 4.13 Proportions of elderly people finding at least one personal, domestic or locomotive task very difficult or impossible who have a home help, by age and gender, people aged 65 and over, Great Britain, 1991

	65–69 years	70–74 years	75–79 years	80–84 years	85–89 years	90 yrs & over	65 yrs & over
	%	%	%	%	%	%	%
Men							
Local Authority home help	11	16	23	(27)	(35)	(50)	23
Private home help	8	4	3	(15)	(12)	(17)	8
N (base)	53	57	66	(48)	(34)	(12)	270
Women							
Local Authority home help	16	22	31	38	44	(35)	31
Private home help	5	6	7	14	17	(7)	10
N (base)	81	100	141	132	86	(43)	583

Source: General Household Survey 1991

Elderly people living alone who had difficulty with at least one personal, domestic or locomotive task were much more likely to have a Local Authority or private home help than those in any other living arrangement (**Table 4.14**). Here, half of those living alone had a Local Authority home help and 13% a private one. Those least likely to have help from Local Authority or private sources were elderly people who lived with a spouse and others.

The gender bias suggested by **Table 4.13** may be because in all age groups, older women are more likely to live alone (see Appendix, **Table 6**). Controlling for age, gender and living arrangements among those who find one of these tasks very difficult or impossible is hampered by small sample sizes. However, of men aged 80 years and over facing these difficulties and living alone, 56% received a Local Authority home help and 25% private help; the corresponding figures for women were 55% and 16%.

Table 4.14 Proportions of elderly people finding at least one personal, domestic or locomotive task very difficult or impossible who have a home help, by living arrangements, people aged 65 and over, Great Britain, 1991

	Lives alone	With spouse only	With spouse and others	With others not spouse
	%	%	%	%
Local Authority home help	50	11	(5)	10
Private home help	13	7	(–)	6
N (base)	386	282	(41)	144

Source: General Household Survey 1991

Help from special facilities, machines or gadgets

If people do not have anyone to help they may manage if they have some other kind of assistance. The 1985 Disability Survey shows the proportions of disabled adults aged 60 and over living in private households who have special furniture, gadgets and adaptations. **Table 4.15** shows that hand rails were the most common adaptations to the home. Twenty-six per cent of women and 18% of men with at least one disability possessed a hand rail in 1985. Bathing aids were also prevalent with half of women and over a third of men with disabilities having these (although as aids to bathing, such as non-slip mats, are relatively cheap and easy to obtain, this is not surprising).

Table 4.15 Proportions of disabled people living in private households with selected aids to independent living, disabled people aged 60 and over, Great Britain, 1985

Has:	Men %	Women %
Special furniture		
none	64	49
bed or bedding aids	12	16
aids to toiletting	6	16
aids to bathing	36	50
other special furniture	9	14
Special gadgets		
none	90	81
utensils	2	6
'pick up' aid	3	8
gadget to summon help	2	4
other special gadgets	5	9
Adaptations		
none	77	70
ramps	3	3
hand rails	18	26
new bathroom/shower	9	8
other home adaptations	6	7
N (weighted)	2,657	4,133
N (unweighted)	2,129	3,108

Source: Disability Survey 1985

Notes: Proportions may sum to more than 100% because some people had more than one special aid.
For explanation of weighting see note to **Table 3.7** in previous chapter.

Very few had special gadgets such as those to summon help (alarms were possessed by only four per cent of women and two per cent of men). Amongst those who did not have aids to independent living, however, many would have liked them (**Table 4.16**). For example, a new bathroom or shower was wanted by 17% of women and 20% of men; aids to bathing by 15% of women and 12% of men; and hand rails by 11% women and nine per cent of men.

Table 4.16 Proportions of disabled people living in private households who would like aids to independent living, but do not have them at present, disabled people aged 60 and over, Great Britain, 1985

	Men	Women
Would like:	%	%
Special furniture		
bed or bedding aids	6	6
aids to toiletting	1	2
aids to bathing	12	15
other special furniture	4	5
needs none or no more	82	77
Special gadgets		
utensils	2	5
'pick up' aid	3	4
gadget to summon help	2	4
other special gadgets	3	6
needs none or no more	91	86
Adaptations		
ramps	2	2
hand rails	9	11
new bathroom/shower	20	17
other home adaptations	9	8
needs none or no more	70	70
N (weighted)	2,657	4,133
N (unweighted)	*2,129*	*3,108*

Source: Disability Survey 1985

Note: proportions may sum to more than 100% because some people wanted more than one special aid

As preparing a hot meal and washing and drying dishes presented problems for some elderly people it is interesting to look at access to consumer durables which might help. Just under two-fifths of people aged 60 and over in 1991 lived in homes where there was a microwave oven, compared with over two-thirds of younger adults (**Table 4.17**). Access to a microwave declined steadily from 57% of those aged 60 to 64 years to 16% of those aged 85–89 years. The proportion of people aged 90 years and over living in households where there was a microwave was 22%.

Table 4.17 Possession of washing machine, microwave oven and dishwasher, by age group, Great Britain, 1991

Household has access to:	60–64 years	65–69 years	70–74 years	75–79 years	80–84 years	85–89 years	90 yrs & over	60 yrs & over	16–59
	%	%	%	%	%	%	%	%	%
Washing machine	93	88	81	74	64	64	60	**82**	**94**
Microwave oven	57	45	34	22	20	16	22	**38**	**68**
Dishwasher	13	8	4	4	4	3	4	**7**	**20**
N (base)	1,218	1,250	939	818	491	211	83	**5,010**	**14,191**

Source: General Household Survey 1991

Table 4.18 Possession of washing machine, microwave oven and dishwasher, by
living arrangement, people aged 60 and over, Great Britain, 1991

Household has access to:	Lives alone	With spouse only	With spouse and others	With others not spouse
	%	%	%	%
Washing machine	63	91	96	85
Microwave oven	23	43	60	41
Dishwasher	2	10	12	9
N (base)	1,637	2,451	455	467

Source: General Household Survey 1991

Elderly people living in households with others were more likely to possess a microwave than those who lived alone (**Table 4.18**).

Proportions owning dishwashers were very small. For those elderly people aged 65 and over living alone who had difficulty washing and drying dishes, only two per cent of women and no men had a dishwasher (General Household Survey 1991, own analysis, table not presented here).

A washing machine may also be helpful to elderly people and is something which many younger households now take for granted. Whereas 94% of people aged 16–59 lived in households with washing machines, the proportion for those aged 60 and over was only 82%. Amongst those aged 60–64 the proportion with washing machines was virtually the same as for people aged 16–59 years but this proportion falls steadily to 60% for those aged 90 years or more. However, as younger generations move into early and late old age, increasing proportions of the oldest age-groups are likely to have access to a washing machine in their own home. Below the age of 60 years, virtually identical proportions of men and women lived in homes with washing machines. Above the age of 60, slightly lower proportions of women (79%) than men (85%) had washing machines (General Household Survey 1991, own analysis, table not presented here). Again this is probably due at least in part to the fact that more women than men from the older generations (who are less likely to have acquired modern consumer durables) have survived. As with microwaves, people were less likely to have a washing machine in the home if they lived alone than if they lived with others.

5

Getting Around For Others

Some key facts*

- nine out of ten people aged 65 or over saw relatives or friends at least once a month

- only two percent of men and women aged 65 or over never saw a friend or relative at all

- half of all men and women aged 65 or over chatted to a neighbour every day

- one-third of people aged 60 and over in 1986 had daily contact with a daughter, compared with one in seven with a son

- at all ages over 69 a higher proportion of men gave help outside their household than women

- over 95% of people aged 55–69 years gave regular practical help in 1988 to someone outside their household

- people aged 55–69 in 1988 were far more likely to *give* help to children and parents than to *receive* help from them

- 14% of men carers and 16% of women carers aged 60 and over in 1990 cared for more than one person

- one carer in five aged 60 and over spent at least 35 hours a week caring in 1990, and one in eight spent at least 100 hours

- one person in six aged 60 and over in 1987 had done some sort of voluntary work in the past year; even in the age group 80–84 years eight per cent of men and women had done some voluntary work

---

* All figures relate to 1991 and to Great Britain unless otherwise stated, and exclude people living in institutions

Discussions about the social circumstances of elderly people often reflect a concern with their isolation, and with the help or care that they need; the fact that older people are usually firmly enmeshed in a supportive social network, and that they often help other people themselves, either on a casual basis or as carers, is frequently forgotten. In this chapter, we deal with two different aspects of 'getting around for others'. We look first at getting around for social purposes: visiting friends and relatives, or simply chatting to neighbours. We then turn to the helping activities of older people, ranging from tasks such as baby-sitting, to caring for others, and voluntary work. The findings are clear: the majority of older people have friends and relatives, visit them regularly, and help them out when the need arises. A significant minority of elderly people, however, are socially isolated and do not have friends or relatives available when they require help.

Getting around for social purposes

In 1991, as in 1985, people aged 65 and over were asked in the General Household Survey 'Do you ever go to see relatives and friends or do relatives and friends come to see you?', and 'Apart from relatives or friends, do you see any of your neighbours to chat to?' They were also asked about the frequency of such visits and chats.

It is clear from **Table 5.1** that most older people see relatives and friends from outside their own household on a regular basis. In 1991 three quarters of people over the age of 65, for example, saw their relatives or friends, and four-fifths saw their neighbours to chat to, at least once a week.

Table 5.1 Frequency of visits to and from relatives and friends, and frequency of seeing neighbours to chat to, people aged 65 and over, Great Britain, 1991

	Relatives or friends	Neighbours
	%	%
Every day/nearly	25	48
2 or 3 times a week	27	23
Once a week	25	11
Less than once a week	21	7
Never	2	11
N (base)	3,773	3,772

Source: General Household Survey 1991

However, more than one in five saw a relative or friend less often than once a week. Of these, over 40% saw a relative or friend less than once a month (eight per cent of the total). Only five per cent neither saw a relative nor friend, nor chatted to a neighbour in the week; and less than half of one per cent never spoke personally to a relative, friend or neighbour at all.

As in 1985 (see Askham et al, 1992:p76), in 1991 there were no significant age differentials in the proportions seeing relatives regularly, although older men were rather more likely to see relatives or friends every day than younger men (**Table 5.2**). Overall, around a quarter of all people aged 65 and over saw relatives or friends every day. However, sex differentials are evident; for example, 21% of men saw a relative or friend every day, compared with 27% of women. Larger proportions of older men in all age groups saw someone less often than once a week, and the proportions rise substantially with age. One man in four aged 65–69 saw someone less than once a week, rising to almost one in three of those aged 90 and over. Overall, more than a quarter of men saw someone less often than once a week. For women, especially the 'young old', the proportions are generally smaller, with

21% overall seeing relatives or friends less than once a week. As with men, the proportions with this low level of contact were considerably higher among very old people: one-third of women aged 90 and over saw relatives or friends less than once a week.

Only two per cent of both men and women never saw a friend or relative at all.

Table 5.2 Frequency of visits to and from relatives and friends, by age group and gender, people aged 65 and over, Great Britain, 1991

	65–69 years	70–74 years	75–79 years	80–84 years	85–89 years	90 yrs & over	65 yrs & over
	%	%	%	%	%	%	%
Men							
every day	22	18	23	19	27	(25)	**21**
2 or 3 times a week	24	27	27	24	23	(38)	**26**
once a week	30	27	23	27	22	(8)	**27**
1 or 2 times a month	13	18	13	16	11	(17)	**14**
less than once a month	9	8	11	11	16	(13)	**10**
never	2	2	4	3	2	(0)	**2**
N (base)	552	415	336	182	64	(24)	**1,573**
Women							
every day	29	25	28	27	27	27	**27**
2 or 3 times a week	26	31	29	28	34	25	**29**
once a week	25	25	21	24	18	16	**23**
1 or 2 times a month	13	11	11	11	12	16	**12**
less than once a month	6	7	9	6	8	13	**7**
never	1	2	3	3	1	4	**2**
N (base)	691	522	478	306	147	56	**2,200**

Source: General Household Survey 1991

Note: Percentages in brackets are based on small numbers and should be used with caution.

Older men were very slightly more likely to say they chatted to neighbours frequently than older women, although the difference is only marked at the oldest ages, and here, for men especially, the sample sizes are very small (**Table 5.3**). Half of men of all ages over 65 chatted to a neighbour every day, and only 17% spoke to a neighbour less than once a week. Just under half of all women spoke to a neighbour every day, although the proportion falls to under one in four for women over 90. Overall, 12% never spoke to a neighbour at all.

Table 5.3 Frequency of seeing neighbours to chat to, by age group and gender, people aged 65 and over, Great Britain, 1991

	65–69 years	70–74 years	75–79 years	80–84 years	85–89 years	90 yrs & over	65 yrs & over
	%	%	%	%	%	%	%
Men							
every day	51	48	55	44	58	(46)	**50**
2 or 3 times a week	24	24	20	20	22	(21)	**23**
once a week	10	12	9	13	3	(13)	**10**
1 or 2 times a month	3	3	4	5	3	(8)	**4**
less than once a month	2	2	1	2	0	(0)	**2**
never	10	11	11	15	14	(13)	**11**
N (base)	550	417	335	182	64	(24)	**1,572**
Women							
every day	48	47	49	47	38	23	**47**
2, 3 times a week	25	25	22	22	20	18	**23**
once a week	11	12	11	14	11	9	**11**
1, 2 times a month	4	3	5	3	7	11	**4**
less than once a month	2	2	2	2	5	2	**2**
never	10	10	12	13	18	39	**12**
N (base)	691	522	478	305	147	57	**2,200**

Source: General Household Survey 1991

Ninety-five per cent of people aged 65–84 chatted to a neighbour or saw a friend or relative at least once a week. It is only at the oldest age group (aged 90 years and over) that the proportion falls to 85%, and three per cent of this age group did not speak to anyone. For all the other age groups, the proportion never seeing anyone was well under one per cent. Although we cannot know anything about the adequacy of social contact from the General Household Survey, only very small proportions seem to be completely socially isolated; it is, however, among the very oldest old that these properties are highest.

Interestingly, however, people who lived alone were more likely to see friends and relatives from outside their own household and chat to neighbours regularly than people who lived with others (**Table 5.4**). A third of people living alone saw someone outside the household every day, compared with only one in ten of those who lived with a spouse and others, and one in five of those who lived with their spouse only.

Table 5.4 Frequency of visits to and from relatives, and frequency of seeing neighbours to chat to, by living arrangements, people aged 65 and over, Great Britain, 1991

	Lives alone	With spouse only	With spouse and others	With others not spouse
	%	%	%	%
Sees relatives/friends:				
every day	32	20	11	26
2 or 3 times a week	28	29	22	21
once a week	21	28	34	18
1 or 2 times a month	9	14	19	18
less than once a month	7	8	13	14
never	3	1	1	3
N (base)	1,419	1,750	224	380
Chats to neighbours:				
every day	50	49	46	37
2 or 3 times a week	23	23	27	19
once a week	10	12	9	11
1 or 2 times a month	3	4	5	6
less than once a month	2	2	1	4
never	12	9	11	24
N (base)	1,419	1,749	224	380

Source: General Household Survey 1991

Over 80% of those living alone saw a friend or relative at least once a week or chatted to a neighbour. The proportion falls to two-thirds for those living with people other than a partner.

To obtain information about *whom* people see, and about social contacts not necessarily involving 'seeing' them, we have to turn to the British Social Attitudes Survey (BSAS) of 1986. This is on a smaller scale than the General Household Survey, but contains far more detailed information about the characteristics of the social relationships of elderly people (see Jarvis, 1993 for more details). People were asked, for example, about the numbers of adult relatives alive, the numbers of close friends alive, and frequency of contact with different family members (see Appendix B, British Social Attitudes Survey, for more detailed information on the questions asked in the special Social Networks and Support Systems Module).

Table 5.5 Numbers of relatives and friends alive, by gender, people aged 60 and over, Great Britain, 1986

	Men	Women	Men & women
	%	%	%
Number of relatives:			
0–4	6	7	**6**
5–9	24	17	**20**
10–19	44	41	**42**
20–29	15	21	**19**
30–39	9	8	**8**
40 or more	4	6	**6**
N (base)	108	140	**248**
Number of close friends:			
0	25	20	**22**
1	8	12	**10**
2	15	15	**15**
3–5	19	24	**22**
6 or more	32	29	**30**
N (base)	130	170	**300**

Source: British Social Attitudes Survey 1986

Only six per cent had fewer than five relatives alive, and the same proportion had more than 40 relatives alive (**Table 5.5**). Two-thirds of the men, and well over half of the women, had between five and 20 relatives alive.

A quarter of men said that they had no close friends, but a third said that they had six or more close friends. Lower proportions of women were found in these extremes, but still one woman in five over the age of 60 said that she had no close friend. Only three per cent overall had fewer than five relatives and friends alive (Jarvis, 1993:p12).

Although this shows that no-one was completely without relatives or friends, simple enumeration of the numbers of family and friends alive provide no indication of the level or type of contact with such people; or, indeed that there was any contact at all.

Respondents were also asked about contact with people in their social networks. As everyone had at least one relative or friend alive, the last column of **Table 5.6** shows the proportion of the whole sample having contact with someone[1]. Seventy-eight per cent actually saw at least one person face-to-face on a daily basis, and as casual acquaintances and neighbours who were not also 'fairly close friends' were explicitly excluded, we can be sure that the large majority of elderly people actually saw people that they were fairly close to on a very regular basis. Only four per cent saw someone face-to-face on a less than monthly basis. The bottom rows of **Table 5.6** ('any daily, any monthly') show the proportions who had any type of contact with relatives or friends – this means actually seeing someone, speaking to them on the telephone, or writing a letter to them. Only 18% of the whole sample did not have any kind of daily contact with another person, and everyone had monthly contact with someone.

---

[1]These figures cannot be compared with the proportions in Table 5.2 seeing relatives and friends every day, because the GHS questions exclude people in the respondent's own household.

Table 5.6 Proportions with specified relatives and friends alive having various levels of contact with them, people aged 60 and over, Great Britain, 1986

Contact with:	Partner	Son	Daughter	Brother	Sister	Any other relative	Friend	Anyone
	%	%	%	%	%	%	%	%
Face-to-face contact								
Daily	100	12	25	3	6	6	14	**78**
At least monthly	–	70	80	25	38	56	82	**96**
Less than monthly	–	31	20	75	62	45	18	**4**
Any contact:								
Daily	100	14	34	3	8	7	14	**82**
At least monthly	–	92	97	39	71	72	88	**100**
Less than monthly	–	8	3	62	29	28	12	**–**
N (Base)	199	202	187	161	175	235	224	**246**

Source: British Social Attitudes Survey 1986

Note: 'any contact' means seeing someone face-to-face, or contact with them by telephone or letter

Over two–thirds of those with sons and daughters actually saw at least one of them on a monthly basis (**Table 5.6**). Over a third of people with daughters had some form of daily contact with a daughter; but only one in seven had similar contact with a son. However, 90% had some form of monthly contact with both sons and daughters. The only network member that the majority did not have monthly contact with was a brother.

Figure 5.1 Frequency of seeing visitors, by gender and disability, people aged 65 and over, Great Britain, 1985 and 1991

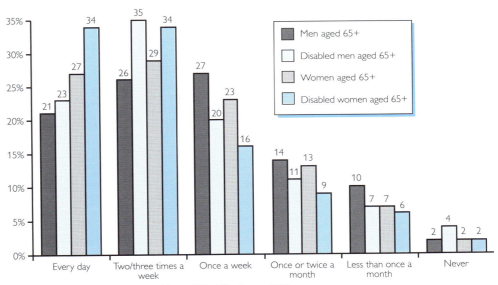

Source: General Household Survey 1991, and Disability Survey 1985

Disabled people form a substantial proportion of the population of older people living in private households (see Introduction). From a comparison between the OPCS Survey of Disabled Adults in Private Households of 1985 (which surveyed only adults with at least one disability) and the General Household Survey of 1991 (which surveyed the general population living in private households), it seems that disabled adults are no more socially isolated than others, at least when analysed by the simple indicator of frequency of seeing visitors (see **Figure 5.1**). However, the questions on social interaction in the two surveys are not truly comparable: the

Disability Survey asked 'How often do you have a visitor or have someone call to see you?', while the General Household Survey, as already noted, asked 'Do you ever go to see relatives and friends or do relatives and friends come to see you?'. The former, therefore, looks only at people who *come* to visit, and could well include people other than friends or relatives (health professionals, for example, are not explicitly excluded). Bearing this in mind, we see that disabled men and women were more likely to have received visitors frequently (every day or two or three times a week) than people in the general population were to see friends or relatives. Forty-seven per cent of men in the general population aged 65 and above saw friends or relatives more than once week, whilst 58% of disabled men of the same age received a visitor more than once a week. The respective proportions for women were 56% and 68%. Under five per cent of all people, whether disabled or in the general population, did not see anyone at all.

Helping others   Almost a third of people over the age of 65 gave help to someone living outside their own household. The General Household Survey did not ask the interviewee to specify which particular task they helped with, though they were prompted, 'if necessary', with tasks such as 'baby-sitting, housework, shopping, gardening, do-it-yourself, or walking the dog'. Nor was there any reference to how often such help was given. The coding notes to the 1991 General Household Survey state that the intention was to find out whether the informant was able to get out and give informal help to others; the respondent could clearly interpret 'help' in any way that he or she chose, although moral support, financial help and voluntary work were specifically omitted.

This time, we find large differences according to both age and gender (**Figure 5.2**).

Figure 5.2 Proportions giving help to someone outside their household, by gender, people aged 65 and over, Great Britain, 1991

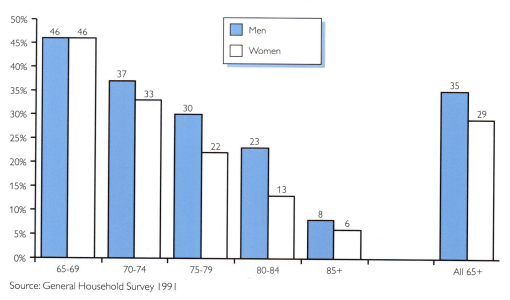

Source: General Household Survey 1991

Overall, 35% of men, but only 29% of women gave help outside the household. Nearly a half of both men and women aged 65–69 years gave some help outside the household, but this proportion declines with age, steadily for men, and more dramatically for women. At all ages after 69 years more men gave help outside the household than women; by the age of 80–84, nearly a quarter of men still gave help outside the household, but only one woman in eight did.

Figure 5.3 Proportions giving help to someone outside their household, by gender and living arrangements, people aged 65 and over, Great Britain, 1991

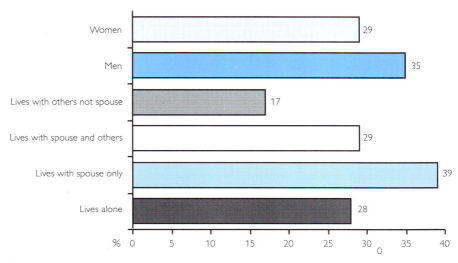

Source: General Household Survey 1991

Overall, 32% of older people gave help outside the household, but proportions vary considerably according to the living arrangements of the person (**Figure 5.3**). Only 17% of those living with someone other than a spouse gave help outside the household, half the proportion of those living with a partner. This is not simply a function of the older age of people living with someone other than a spouse (see Chapter 4 above), but probably also of factors such as health.

An analysis of the Retirement Survey of 1988, which examines the situation of a rather younger group of people (people aged 55–69 only), shows much larger proportions 'regularly or frequently' helping others out. It should be noted that this help was not necessarily given to people *outside* the household. Respondents were given a list of tasks (see **Figure 5.4**), and asked it they regularly or frequently did any of the things listed for their children, parents, any other relative, or anyone else.

Figure 5.4 Proportions regularly or frequently giving help to at least one other person, by gender, people aged 55–69, Great Britain, 1988

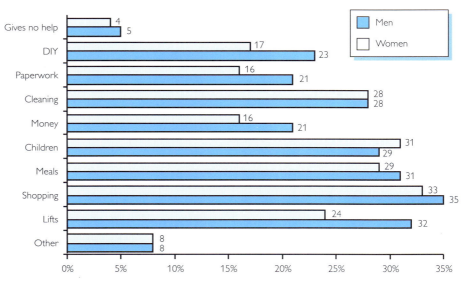

Source: Retirement Survey 1988

Only five per cent of men and four per cent of women gave no help to anyone; over 95%, then, gave some sort of practical help to another person on a frequent or regular basis. We see again that for almost all tasks a higher proportion of men helped out than women. This is true even of traditionally 'female' tasks. For example, a third of women helped someone out with the shopping, compared with 35% of men; and 29% of women helped someone with meals, compared with 31% of men. The only task that a higher proportion of women helped out with was looking after children, and even here the difference was small – 31% of women, compared with 29% of men (**Table 5.7**).

Table 5.7 Proportions regularly or frequently giving help to specified relative/friend, by type of help given and gender, people aged 55–69, Great Britain, 1988

	Children	Parents	Other relatives	Other	Anyone
	%	%	%	%	%
Men					
no relative/friend	16	66	11	11	0
gives no help	33	16	75	70	5
helps out with:					
lifts in car	17	8	6	10	32
shopping	17	12	5	9	35
meals	23	6	3	2	31
children	28	0	1	1	29
money	18	3	2	1	21
cleaning	21	7	2	1	28
paper work	10	8	3	3	21
DIY	13	7	3	4	23
other	2	2	1	4	8
N (base)	1,628	1,628	1,628	1,628	**1,628**
Women					
no relative/friend	15	71	13	11	0
gives no help	36	14	72	70	4
helps out with:					
lifts in car	12	5	5	9	24
shopping	14	10	6	9	33
meals	20	6	4	2	29
children	29	15	1	1	31
money	13	2	1	1	16
cleaning	19	7	4	2	28
paper work	6	6	3	3	16
DIY	9	5	3	3	17
other	2	2	1	4	8
N (base)	1,806	1,806	1,806	1,806	**1,806**

Source: Retirement Survey 1988

Fairly large proportions of the sample of people aged 55–69 did not have certain relatives or friends alive (16% of men, for example, did not have children, whilst 71% of women no longer had parents alive), but everyone had someone – a child, parent, other relative or friend – to whom they could, potentially, give help (final column, **Table 5.7**). Whilst we find that fairly large proportions of the sample did not give help to each category of friend or relative (a third, for example, gave no help to their offspring, whilst three quarters gave no help to relatives other than children or parents), overall, however, almost everyone gave help to someone.

It is noteworthy that at this 'younger' end of later life, people were more likely to give than to receive help (**Table 5.8**).

Table 5.8 Proportions giving and receiving help from children and parents, by gender, people aged 55–69, Great Britain, 1988

	Men	Women
	%	%
Help given to children	50	48
Help received from children	24	32
Help reciprocated	19	22
Help given to parents	18	14
Help received from parents	1	1
Help reciprocated	1	1
N (base)	1,628	1,806

Source: Retirement Survey 1988

Half of the sample of men gave some sort of help to a son or daughter, but only a quarter received help from a child. In only one case in five did a man both give and receive help from a child. Women were more likely to receive help from a child (32%), and slightly more likely both to give and receive help (22%). Only minorities of men and women aged between 55 and 69 had parents alive, and only 18% of men and 14% of women in the whole sample helped out a parent. Very few parents (almost all of whom must have been over the age of 75) helped out their children, and in only one per cent of the whole sample did parents and their own elderly offspring help each other out.

Caring for others
We now turn to the more specific kind of help involved in looking after people who cannot manage on their own. A special section on carers was included in the 1990 General Household Survey (see OPCS 1992a for details and useful tabulations). The section was intended to cover people who look after chronically sick, handicapped or elderly people, whether relatives or non-relatives, adults or children. It also included people who help others out with shopping or odd jobs, so long as the service was provided regularly to a sick, handicapped or elderly person.

Figure 5.5 Proportions caring for at least one sick, elderly or handicapped person, by age group and gender, Great Britain, 1990

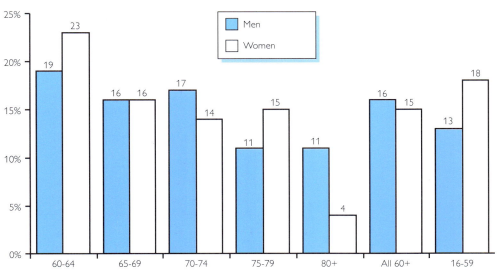

Source: General Household Survey 1990

Not surprisingly, smaller proportions of people were caring for someone than simply helping out on a regular basis, but even so in 1990, one person in seven aged 60 or over was caring for someone who either lived in or outside their household. Even at the age of 80 and over, one person in sixteen was caring for someone. Two things are clear from **Figure 5.5**. Firstly, there is not a great deal of difference between people over 60 and people under 60. Overall, 16% of people under 60 were caring for someone, compared with 15% of people over 60. Secondly, sex differentials are far less clear cut than for merely giving help to someone, but older men were still slightly more likely to be caring for someone than older women (though numerically, of course, there are far more women than men carers). At the age of 80 and over, three times the proportion of men were carers than women. In the younger age groups, particularly those aged under 60 and those aged 60–64, larger proportions of women were carers than men; the differentials are greatest under the age of 60, with 18% of women caring, compared with 13% of men.

The majority of carers looked after someone who did not live with them, so their caring was a reason for getting out and about. However, people aged 60 and over were more likely than younger adults to be caring for someone living with them and less likely to be looking after someone living elsewhere. Six per cent of older people were 'co-resident' carers compared with three per cent of younger people. The proportion of those aged 60 or more who looked after someone whom they did not live with was 10% compared with 12% for people aged 16–59. Not surprisingly people in their sixties were more likely to be non co–resident carers than those in older age groups (**Figure 5.6**). Seventeen per cent of women aged 60–64 and 13% of men in the same age group were getting out of the home to care for someone not living with them. At older ages the proportion falls. The incidence of co-resident caring was highest of all among men aged 80 or older, of whom one in twelve (8%) was looking after someone living with him. The corresponding proportion for women aged 80 and over was just two per cent. This difference is due largely to differences in marital status and living arrangements (see Appendix **Tables A.5** and **A.6**); higher proportions of men than women are married and living with their spouses when they are in their eighties and nineties.

Figure 5.6 Proportions caring for at least one sick, elderly or handicapped person
by whether co-resident or not, age group and gender, Great Britain, 1990

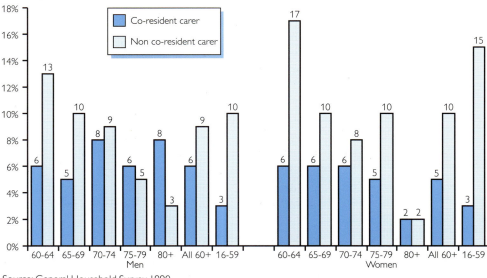

Source: General Household Survey 1990

Note: Those caring for someone who lives with them *and* someone who lives elsewhere are counted as co-resident carers and not non co-resident carers

Table 5.9 Total number of people cared for, by gender, carers aged 16–59 and 60 and over, Great Britain, 1990

	Aged 60 years and over:			Aged 16–59 years:		
	men	women	men & women	men	women	men & women
	%	%	%	%	%	%
1	86	83	**84**	78	78	**78**
2	13	13	**13**	18	18	**18**
3	1	3	**2**	3	3	**3**
4 or more	0	0	**0**	1	1	1
Mean	1.16	1.22	**1.19**	1.28	1.27	**1.28**
N (base)	327	411	**738**	765	1,212	**1,977**

Source: General Household Survey 1990

The gender differences in the numbers of people cared for and hours spent caring are not large (**Table 5.9**). Over 80% of both male and female carers aged 60 and over cared for only one person; a further 13% cared for two people. One per cent of men, and three per cent of women, cared for three or more people.

Table 5.10 Total number of hours a week spent caring, by gender, carers aged 16–59 and 60 and over, Great Britain, 1990

	Aged 60 years and over:			Aged 16–59 years:		
	men	women	men & women	men	women	men & women
	%	%	%	%	%	%
under 5 hours	34	29	**32**	40	30	**34**
5–9 hours	18	23	**21**	26	25	**26**
10–34 hours	20	22	**21**	23	29	**26**
35–99 hours	10	8	**9**	5	7	**6**
100 hours or more	12	14	**13**	2	6	**5**
varies	5	4	**5**	4	3	**4**
N (base)	322	405	**727**	764	1,208	**1,972**

Source: General Household Survey 1990

Men *under* the age of 60 were far less likely than women to spend substantial weekly amounts of time caring (**Table 5.10**). Forty per cent spent less than five hours a week caring, compared with 30% of women, and the proportion of women who spent at least 35 hours a week caring was twice that for men. Two thirds of men and more than half the women under 60 spent under ten hours a week caring. Men and women over 60, however, spent more substantial amounts of time every week caring for someone. One carer in five spent at least 35 hours a week caring, and one carer in eight spent a hundred hours or more a week caring. Differences in the number of hours men and women over the age of 60 spent caring were very small compared with those found for younger carers.

Voluntary work In 1987 about one person in six aged 60 and over undertook some sort of voluntary work in the previous year; this covers activities ranging from collecting money and giving advice to serving on a committee and organising entertainment. Although roughly the same proportions of men and women over 60 did voluntary work, young elderly people were far more likely to do so, with 26% of women aged 60–69 undertaking voluntary work, compared with only 20% of men. Even in the age group 80–84 years, however, eight per cent of men and women did some kind of voluntary work (**Figure 5.7**).

Figure 5.7 Proportions undertaking voluntary work in the past twelve months, by age and gender, Great Britain, 1987

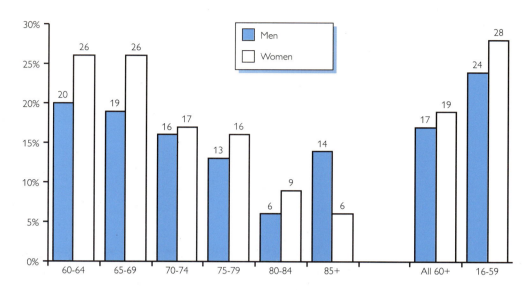

Source: General Household Survey 1987

Although rather lower proportions of both men and women aged 60 and over undertook voluntary work compared with people under 60, those who did invested much more substantial amounts of time in such work (**Table 5.11**).

Table 5.11 Number of days in past year spent doing voluntary work, by gender, people aged 16–59 and 60 and over, Great Britain, 1987

| | Aged 60 years and over: | | Aged 16–59 years: | |
| | **Men** | **Women** | **Men** | **Women** |
	%	%	%	%
1–5 days	16	17	25	26
6–9 days	10	8	13	13
10–19 days	12	14	13	13
20–49 days	20	22	19	23
50–99 days	19	21	14	15
100 days or more	23	19	16	12
N (base)	349	559	1,572	1,967

Source: General Household Survey 1987

People were asked to estimate how many days they had spent doing any kind of voluntary work with a group in the last twelve months, and were prompted with the above categories if necessary. Only a quarter of volunteers aged 60 and over spent fewer than ten days volunteering; two-fifths of volunteers under the age of 60 did so. Similarly, two-fifths of volunteers aged 60 and over spent 50 or more days volunteering, compared with less than a third of volunteers under 60.

6

Getting around outside the home

Some key facts*

- three-quarters of people aged 65 and over had no difficulty getting out of doors and walking down the road, but one-fifth of the men in this age group and a quarter of the women found it quite difficult, very difficult or impossible

- 72% of people aged 65 and over had no difficulty doing the household shopping on their own, but there were strong gender differences: 80% of men, but only 66% of women, had no difficulty doing the household shopping on their own; 14% of men and 25% of women found it very difficult or impossible

- only a half of all disabled men aged 65 and over living in private households in 1985 could manage the shopping on their own without difficulty, and a third found it impossible; only a third of disabled women aged 65 and over could manage the shopping without difficulty, and two-fifths found it impossible

- just over half of all people aged 65 and over lived in households without access to a car

- over 80% of older people who lived alone were without access to a car

- over two-thirds of people aged 65 and over who did not have household access to a car were able to use public transport on their own, but 30% did not use public transport at all

- 7% of all men aged 65 and over, and 13% of the women, were bound to their immediate locality by having no access to a car at all (either within or outside their household) combined with a health problem that prevented them using public transport

- over two-thirds of disabled people aged 65 and over in 1985 said that their disability prevented them from going out as often as they would like, and the main problem was that their disability caused them too much effort or pain

***All figures relate to Great Britain and to 1991 unless otherwise stated, and exclude people living in institutions.**

The ability to get about outside the home is vital for a variety of purposes: exercise, work, the pursuit of necessary tasks such as shopping, and maintaining a sense of community with friends and neighbours in the outside world. The ability to get further afield, whether by car or public transport, can be essential for maintaining physical contact with friends and relatives in other parts of the town or country, and for visiting interesting places in leisure time. Most people need and wish to get out and about, but the special problems posed by disabling conditions mean that not everyone can get out of doors on their own. In this chapter, we examine the ability of the older population living in private households to get around the immediate neighbourhood, and to travel further afield. We also focus on the special problems faced by disabled people living in the community.

Getting around the neighbourhood

We have seen in Chapter Four that the vast majority of elderly people had no difficulty at all in undertaking basic domestic and personal care tasks for themselves. We see from **Table 6.1**, however, that far higher proportions, especially of women, had difficulty doing the simplest task that would get them **out and about** – getting out of doors and walking down the road unaided. The General Household Survey of 1991 found that one man in five aged 65 and over, and 27% of women, found it quite difficult, very difficult, or impossible, to get out of doors and walk down the road alone. The proportions having some degree of difficulty getting out of doors rose sharply with age. Whilst only six per cent of people aged 65–69 years found it very difficult or impossible to get out of doors, almost half (48%) the people aged 85 and over found it similarly difficult.

Not surprisingly, people who had difficulty getting out of doors on their own also had difficulty doing the household shopping on their own; but while roughly the same proportions of men found it difficult to get out of the house and to do the household shopping, considerably larger proportions of women found it difficult to do the household shopping. A fifth of men aged 65 and over had some degree of difficulty doing the shopping, compared with a third of women. The difficulty experienced by very old women in doing household shopping on their own (compared with both the proportions of very old men finding difficulty doing the household shopping, and those same women getting out of doors and walking down the road) may well be related to the very small proportions of very old women who have access to a car and are able to drive[1]. (For more information on access to cars, see *Going further afield*, below in this chapter.)

---

[1] **The question asks about the ability of people to do the household shopping on their own, but does not distinguish between shopping on foot and shopping by car.**

Table 6.1 Proportions able to walk down the road, and to do the household shopping on their own, by age group and gender, people aged 65 and over, Great Britain, 1991

	65–69 years	70–74 years	75–79 years	80–84 years	85–89 years	90 yrs & over	65 yrs & over
	%	%	%	%	%	%	%
Men							
Getting out of doors and walking down the road							
not difficult	88	86	77	70	40	(38)	**80**
quite difficult	6	9	12	14	17	(25)	**10**
very difficult	4	3	5	9	16	(21)	**5**
impossible	2	2	5	7	27	(17)	**5**
Doing the household shopping on own							
not difficult	88	85	76	66	43	(42)	**80**
quite difficult	6	6	6	8	5	(0)	**6**
very difficult	2	3	6	8	14	(21)	**5**
impossible	4	5	11	18	38	(38)	**9**
N (base)	552	417	336	183	63	(24)	**1,575**
Women							
Getting out of doors and walking down the road							
not difficult	87	81	69	57	37	21	**72**
quite difficult	7	8	15	19	18	13	**11**
very difficult	3	5	8	11	18	16	**7**
impossible	3	5	9	13	26	50	**9**
Doing the household shopping on own							
not difficult	82	74	64	49	29	9	**66**
quite difficult	7	10	10	11	10	11	**9**
very difficult	5	5	10	12	13	4	**8**
impossible	7	11	16	28	48	77	**17**
N (base)	690	522	478	306	147	56	**2,199**

Source: General Household Survey 1991

Note: Percentages in brackets are based on small numbers and should be used with caution.

By age 85 and over, 76% of women, but only 57% of men, had some degree of difficulty doing the shopping on their own. Overall, one man in ten, and one woman in six, aged 65 and over found it impossible to do the shopping.

The picture already seen in Chapter Four is again evident here when we examine the proportions having difficulty getting out and about by living arrangements (**Table 6.2**). However, considerably higher proportions in all types of household find it impossible to do the household shopping alone, than found it impossible to do the hardest task *within* the house (get up and down the stairs unaided). One person in four living alone found it very difficult or impossible to do the household shopping on their own, whilst 41% of those living with others (but not with spouse) found it very difficult or impossible.

Table 6.2 Proportions able to walk down the road, and to do the household shopping on their own, by living arrangement, people aged 65 and over, Great Britain, 1991

	Lives alone	With spouse only	With spouse and others	With others not spouse
	%	%	%	%
Getting out of doors and walking down the road				
not difficult	73	81	80	59
quite difficult	12	9	11	14
very difficult	7	5	4	11
impossible	8	5	4	17
Doing the household shopping on own				
not difficult	69	79	74	50
quite difficult	8	7	12	9
very difficult	8	5	4	9
impossible	15	10	10	32
N (base)	1,420	1,751	224	379

Source: General Household Survey 1991

The overall picture is of considerable proportions of elderly people unable to get out of the house on their own. Of the 13% of all elderly people who found it very difficult or impossible to get out of the house on their own, three quarters (76%) said they needed help to get out of the house and walk down the road, whilst five per cent (well under one per cent of all elderly people) found it impossible, even with help. Of the 20% of all elderly people who found it very difficult or impossible to do the household shopping, 95% needed help to do it, and two per cent found it impossible, even with help (General Household Survey 1991, own analysis, table not presented here).

It is disturbing to note that around 15% of the elderly people who lived alone found it very difficult or impossible to get outside on their own, and almost a quarter found it very difficult or impossible to do their own shopping. Of these, 73% were reliant on help outside their home to get out of the house, and six per cent could not manage it, even with help. Ninety-five per cent were reliant on help outside the home to do their shopping, and two per cent could not manage it at all. Overall, 97% of the people living alone who found it very difficult or impossible to do their own shopping, had to rely on someone outside their own home for their very existence (General Household Survey 1991, own analysis, table not presented here).

Going further afield   It is not easy to get outside the immediate locality without access to transport. In particular, a car provides easy and quick access to the outside world, and cars can be specially adapted for disabilities. Even people who have difficulty climbing stairs or walking down the road may find that a car provides them with a means – and perhaps the *only* means – of visiting friends or leisure facilities. The majority of elderly people, however, unlike people under the age of 65, in 1991 lived in households that did not have access to a car (**Figure 6.1**).

Figure 6.1 Proportions living in a household with access to a car, by age group and gender, Great Britain, 1991

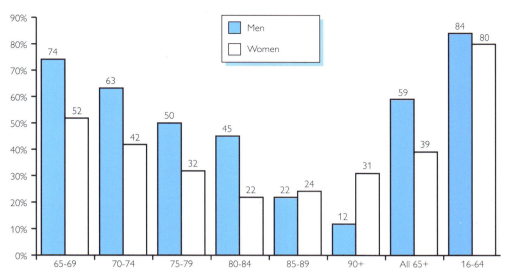

Source: General Household Survey 1991

Access to a car is strongly age-related and strongly gender-specific over the age of 65. Between the ages of 16 and 64, over 80% of both men and women had access to a car, but from age 65–69 onwards, the gender differentials begin to widen. In 1991 three in every four men aged 65–69 had access to a car, compared with only one woman in two. By age 75–79, one in two men had access to a car, compared with one woman in three. At age 85 and over, only one person in four overall had household access to a car.

Gender differentials, except for those living alone, are not as pronounced when we look at access to cars by living arrangements (this is not surprising, as we can only look at household access to cars, and most households containing more than one person will be composed of both men and women). However, the difference between people living alone and others is startling (**Table 6.3**).

Table 6.3 Proportions living in a household with access to a car, by gender and living arrangements, people aged 65 and over, Great Britain, 1991

	Lives alone	With spouse only	With spouse and others	With others not spouse
	%	%	%	%
Men	36	66	79	60
N (base)	373	974	143	94
Women	12	63	72	59
N (base)	1,049	787	85	291

Source: General Household Survey 1991

While just under half of all people aged 65 and over, and more than two thirds of those living in households with more than one person, had access to a car, only one man in three living alone, and one woman in eight living alone, had a car. Overall, 82% of people aged 65 and over living alone did not have a car.

Figure 6.2 Proportions living alone with access to a car, by age group and gender, people aged 65 and over, Great Britain, 1991

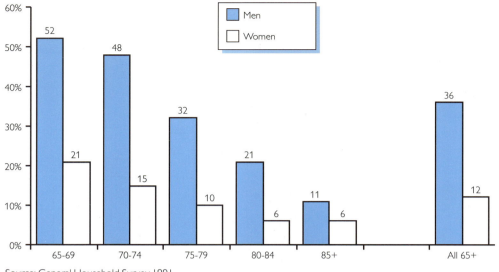

Source: General Household Survey 1991

Only small minorities of women at all ages living alone had a car (**Figure 6.2**). By the age of 80–84, only six per cent had a car, compared with 21% of men.

For the 53% of all elderly people without household access to a car, the ability to use public transport is vital for travelling outside the immediate locality. **Table 6.4** shows the use of public transport by people aged 65 and over who did not have household access to a car.

Table 6.4 Use of public transport by people who do not have household access to a car, by age group and gender, people aged 65 and over, Great Britain, 1991

	65–69 years	70–74 years	75–79 years	80–84 years	85 yrs & over	65 yrs & over
	%	%	%	%	%	%
Men use public transport:						
on own	84	75	72	60	36	**70**
with help	3	2	4	5	3	**3**
not at all	12	23	24	35	61	**27**
N (base)	145	156	167	99	72	**639**
Women use public transport:						
on own	83	76	64	46	27	**64**
with help	4	4	7	7	6	**5**
not at all	14	20	29	47	67	**31**
N (base)	332	305	327	237	152	**1,353**

Source: General Household Survey 1991

Seventy per cent of men and nearly two-thirds of women used public transport on their own, and further small percentages used it with the help of someone else. This still leaves, however, almost a third of people aged 65 and over living in households without a car who did not use public transport.

Table 6.5 Use of public transport by people living alone without a car, by gender, people aged 65 and over, 1991

	Men	Women	Men & women
	%	%	%
Uses public transport:			
on own	69	63	**65**
with help	2	4	**4**
not at all	29	33	**32**
N (base)	239	922	**1,161**

Source: General Household Survey 1991

Similarly, of those living alone without a car (**Table 6.5**), just over a third did not use public transport at all.

Overall, one person in seven over the age of 65 did not have a car and did not use public transport, a sizeable proportion apparently without any easy access to places outside their immediate locality.

Table 6.6 Reasons for not using public transport of people living in households without access to a car, by gender, people aged 65 and over, Great Britain, 1991

	Men	Women
	%	%
Health/physical difficulty	62	72
Private transport	36	25
Too expensive	3	3
Inconvenient	8	11
Other	–	2
N (base)	172	413

Source: General Household Survey 1991

Note: percentages sum to more than 100% because some people had more than one reason for not using public transport

As **Table 6.6** shows, however, a quarter of women and a third of men without household access to a car did not use public transport because they had access to private transport, (presumably many from relatives or friends). Yet for the large majority the reason for not using public transport was that a health problem or physical difficulty precluded it. Only a small minority found it too inconvenient, and only three per cent found it too expensive. Overall, seven per cent of older men and 13% of older women did not have a car and were effectively bound to their immediate locality by a health problem that meant they could not use public transport.

Getting around with a disability

As noted in the Introduction, around one adult in seven living in a private household has at least one disability, a proportion that rises sharply with age. Although the special section of the General Household Survey on people aged 65 and over contains detailed information on the ability of the older population to perform many tasks (see Chapter Four), the General Household Survey by definition examines the general population, and is not suited to a detailed study of the disabled population. The OPCS Disability Surveys, however, only interviewed people with at least one disability, enabling us to answer interesting questions concerning the ability of the disabled population living in private households to get around outside the home. Does disability severely restrict the ability of people to get around, or do most people manage to get out and about in spite of difficulties? If people cannot get out and about, what prevents them from doing so?

Table 6.7 Proportions of disabled people able to do the household shopping on their own, by age group and gender, disabled people aged 65 and over, Great Britain, 1985

	65–69 years	70–74 years	75–79 years	80–84 years	85 yrs & over	65 yrs & over
	%	%	%	%	%	%
Men						
not difficult	55	56	48	38	25	**49**
quite difficult	11	10	14	13	9	**12**
very difficult	8	11	8	10	15	**10**
impossible	26	22	30	38	51	**30**
N (base)	537	571	489	314	163	**2,074**
N (unweighted)	460	493	390	246	113	**1,702**
Women						
not difficult	36	38	33	24	8	**29**
quite difficult	21	19	17	15	8	**16**
very difficult	15	14	14	11	10	**13**
impossible	28	30	35	50	73	**42**
N (base)	630	795	895	751	569	**3,639**
N (unweighted)	531	663	715	549	382	**2,340**

Source: Disability Survey 1985

Note: for explanation of weighted and unweighted samples see Table 3.7, Chapter 3

It is immediately clear, comparing **Tables 6.7** and **6.1**, that far larger proportions of disabled people aged 65 or over find it difficult or impossible to do the household shopping than the general population of people aged 65 and over. Eighty per cent of all men aged 65 and over in 1991 found it not at all difficult to do the household shopping alone, and only one in ten found it impossible. Only a half of all disabled older men in 1985, however, could manage the shopping without difficulty, and almost a third found it impossible. Two thirds of all women over 65 could manage the shopping easily, and around one in five found it impossible; under one in three disabled women could manage the shopping easily, however, and over 40% could not manage it at all on their own. Over the age of 85, half of disabled men and three quarters of disabled women found it impossible to do the household shopping on their own. More disabled women of all ages over 65 than men found it very difficult or impossible to do the shopping.

Not surprisingly, the ability to do tasks easily is heavily dependent on the severity of disability[2].

---

[2] See Appendix B, Surveys of Disability, *Surveys used in this report,* for notes on the construction of severity scores, and examples.

Only two per cent of men and five per cent of women in the lowest severity category (**Figure 6.3**) found it impossible to do the household shopping on their own, but the proportions rose sharply with degree of severity until, within severity category ten, everyone found it impossible to do the household shopping on their own. Interestingly, the gender differentials in the different severity categories are not particularly large, although in almost all the severity categories slightly larger proportions of women found it impossible to do the household shopping. The reason why much larger proportions of disabled women overall found it very difficult or impossible to do tasks when compared with men is that women tend to be more severely disabled than men (only one disabled woman in seven was in severity category one, compared with one in four men; 37% of men were severely disabled – severity category five and above – compared with 48% of women; see **Table A.12** in Appendix A).

Around two-thirds of disabled people of all ages over 65 stated that their health problem or disability prevented them from going out as often or as far as they would like (**Table 6.8**); interestingly, there are no clear gender differentials, and the proportions do not rise rapidly with age. Indeed, only 56% of men aged 85 and over said that their ability to get about outside the home was limited by their health or functional impairment.

Figure 6.3 Proportions of disabled people finding it impossible to do the household shopping on their own, by gender and severity category, disabled people aged 65 and over, Great Britain, 1985

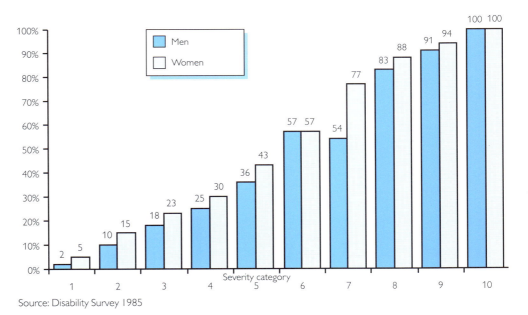

Source: Disability Survey 1985

Table 6.8 Proportions of disabled people whose health problem or disability prevents them from going out as often or as far as they would like, by gender, disabled people aged 65 and over, Great Britain, 1985

	65–69 years	70–74 years	75–79 years	80–84 years	85 yrs & over	65 yrs & over
	%	%	%	%	%	%
Men	65	66	65	62	56	**64**
N (weighted)	515	531	429	262	124	**1,862**
N (unweighted)	424	426	321	179	76	**1,426**
Women	67	66	69	73	69	**69**
N (weighted)	593	741	797	630	366	**3,126**
N (unweighted)	483	590	599	425	217	**2,314**

Source: Disability Survey 1985

The reason for this is clear from **Figure 6.4.** Although severity of impairment rises rapidly with age, the proportions saying that their disability prevents them from going out more often rises only slowly with severity of disability. Indeed, apart from the least disabled people, where only 35% of men and 40% of women said that their disability prevented them from going out more often, the proportions giving this answer in the severity categories are much the same (and high). At least two-thirds, and generally more than three-quarters of disabled men and women in all severity categories above category one did not get outside the home as often as they wanted because of their disability. Large numbers of disabled older people, then, whether mildly or severely affected, do not get outside the home as often as they would like.

Figure 6.4 Proportions of disabled people whose disability prevents them going out as often as they would like, by gender and severity category, disabled people aged 65 and over, Great Britain, 1985

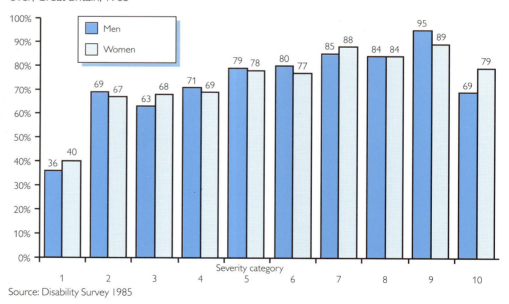

Source: Disability Survey 1985

Table 6.9 What prevents restricted disabled people from going out more often or further afield? by age group and gender, disabled people aged 65 and over whose disability/health prevents them going out as often as they would like, Great Britain, 1985

	65–69 years	70–74 years	75–79 years	80–84 years	85 yrs & over	65 yrs & over
	%	%	%	%	%	%
Men						
transport problems	18	19	19	21	(31)	**20**
access problems	5	8	5	4	(7)	**6**
no-one to go with	6	6	10	13	(11)	**8**
too much effort or pain	74	74	64	75	(81)	**72**
no confidence/fear	14	12	13	13	(6)	**13**
can't afford it	10	9	8	4	(4)	**8**
other reasons	15	11	9	8	(19)	**12**
N (weighted)	332	350	277	163	(70)	**1,192**
N (unweighted)	271	279	206	111	(41)	**908**
Women						
transport problems	22	23	21	24	30	**23**
access problems	5	10	6	5	5	**6**
no-one to go with	10	15	16	22	24	**17**
too much effort or pain	77	76	73	69	65	**72**
no confidence/fear	20	15	18	20	20	**14**
can't afford it	8	4	5	1	2	**4**
other reasons	10	8	7	10	10	**9**
N (weighted)	400	489	547	458	250	**2,144**
N (unweighted)	325	383	406	304	145	**1,563**

Source: Disability Survey 1985

Note: columns sum to more than 100% because some people had more than one reason for not going out more.

There are clearly no simple solutions (**Table 6.9**). Older disabled people had a variety of reasons for not getting out as often as they would like, and most had more than one reason for not getting out. The overwhelming reason, however, in all age groups, was simply that getting out took too much effort or caused too much pain. Substantial proportions, especially among the 'old elderly', found transport a problem, and a quarter of disabled women over the age of 85 did not get out as often as they wished because they had no-one with whom to go.

7

Summary

Like other adult age groups most older people can get around to look after themselves and their homes without any difficulty (Chapter Four). However, either their own health or their housing facilities makes this more difficult for some than others. **Women,** for example, are slightly more likely than men to live in a flat rather than a whole house (22% compared with 16% of men), and although in some ways this could be an advantage, they are also more likely than men to live in a flat not at ground level and without a lift. They are more likely to have some difficulty with both personal care and domestic tasks, and particularly likely to find at least one domestic task either very difficult or impossible. Fortunately, they are more likely than men to get a home help if they have difficulty with personal, domestic or locomotive tasks (reflecting the fact that frail or disabled older women are more likely to be on their own than similarly placed men). Disabled women are also more likely than disabled men to have special furniture, gadgets or adaptations around the house.

People who **live alone** are also at a disadvantage in getting around at home compared to some others. For example, they are more likely to have difficulty with domestic and locomotive tasks than those who live with a spouse, and more likely to find at least one task very difficult or impossible. The only group which has more difficulty is those who live with other people, not their spouse, and this group would include people who have such a living arrangement precisely because they have difficulty managing on their own. Those who live alone are the group least likely to have the assistance of a washing machine, a microwave, or a dishwasher. Because more of them lack this human or mechanical help in the house, those who live alone are the group most likely to receive a local authority or private home help when they cannot manage personal, domestic or locomotive tasks for themselves.

Thirdly, the **very old** are at a clear disadvantage compared with younger elderly people. Those over eighty are less likely to have central heating, access to a car, a washing machine or a microwave than younger people. Yet their need for an assisted domestic environment is considerable since the capacity to cope with all domestic, personal and locomotive tasks (at least those enquired about in the General Household Survey) declines markedly with age, and increasingly steeply after the age of eighty.

Not only can older people generally help themselves without difficulty, they also clearly have the capacity to get out and about to talk to and help others (Chapter Five). The vast majority have at least five living adult friends and/or relatives, have daily contact of some sort with someone, and *see* someone to talk to at least once a week. Eighty-five percent have children, and if these are daughters, one-third of their older parents have some sort of contact with them daily. In addition, at least for young elderly people (55–69 years), this contact is much more likely to involve the parents helping the children than vice-versa. It is not only children who are helped of course; all but a tiny minority of *younger* older people give some practical help to someone on a regular basis, and a third of *all* older people give help to someone outside their household. About one-sixth are also involved in voluntary work. Understandably smaller proportions help to look after someone who cannot manage on his or her own, but even so, one in seven older people has caring responsibilities (more often for someone outside their household) and these take up more of their time than for carers under the age of sixty.

As with other activities the ability to get out and about for others clearly declines with age, and there are also sex differences which probably reflect the older age, and less healthy profile of women.

It is also clear that most of the older population get out and about for leisure purposes (Chapter Three), and such trend data as we have suggest that older people may well be becoming more active. However, the most common leisure pursuit is television-watching, and there are many older people whose leisure activities are largely taken at home. This is particularly true of the **disabled old**, among whom there are disturbingly high proportions doing nothing and not going out. Men seem to be more active in leisure pursuits than women, for example more likely to go for walks, to cycle, to take part in physically active sports. Yet this may to some extent be an artefact of the kinds of pursuits investigated; when moderate to vigorous activity in the home is included (such as housework and caring activities) women seem no less active than men. Participation in leisure activities clearly declines with age, with those in very late life being much less likely than the young old to read, listen to the radio, garden, travel for leisure, take holidays, etc. However, there are still sizeable proportions in the later age groups who do participate in these activities, just as there are many in the younger ages who do not. Both health and income are implicated in accounting for non-participation, though complex causal analysis cannot be provided through these kinds of data.

Older people, of course, get around for work far less than younger people, and the trend towards earlier retirement has continued for men (Chapter Two). This difference between younger and older people is signified by the much smaller average distances travelled for work purposes by older people. Also. because they are less likely to work (and when they do, often work shorter hours and for lower rates of pay) their incomes are lower, which may affect their getting around for other purposes.

However, it should not be overlooked that sizeable though small proportions of older people *do* get around for work, especially in the first few years after state pension age.

Helping other people, as well as looking after themselves, enjoying leisure, working or visiting friends and relatives, obviously takes older people out of doors both within their neighbourhood and further afield (Chapter Six). For active older people this is unproblematic; they have no major health problems to deter them, and many have access to a car. However, again it is important to distinguish between the active majority and those who do have difficulty. Disabled older people are more likely to have difficulty, as are women, those who live alone, and the older old. For example disabled older people are much more likely to have difficulty doing the household shopping and the majority say that their disability prevents them going out as often or as far as they would like.

Women, apart from their older age profile than men are also, from age seventy-five upwards, more likely to be disabled, and if they are disabled are more likely to be severely disabled. It is therefore not surprising to find their ability to get out and about more restricted than that of men; this is partly due to physical inability and partly to their more limited access to cars. Similarly, the older old have more difficulty than the younger old, so that by the time people reach their mid-eighties the *majority* have difficulty getting out of doors and doing the shopping, and have neither household access to a car, nor use public transport on their own.

The summary table (**Table 7.1**) shows how active the older population is in basic activities, but also how, the more demanding the activities, the more they are likely to be a minority pursuit, predominantly carried out by younger older people. Both young elderly and very elderly women are less active than elderly men in the same age groups in all the main activities covered in our survey data, except that young elderly women are somewhat *less* likely than young elderly men to have a limiting long-standing illness, slightly more likely to have done voluntary work, and just as likely to be active as caregivers.

There are very substantial differences between younger and older elderly people, with only very small proportions of the latter – especially amongst the women – active beyond their own domestic and family lives. Although it is clear that as men and women reach very late life their activities become more circumscribed, in earlier late life their mobility and task capacity are unimpaired and show them well able to be involved beyond their own home and household, in work, caregiving, sport and recreations.

Table 7.1 How active is the older population?

	Men		Women	
	60/65*–79 years	80 years & over	60/65*–79 years	80 years & over
	%	%	%	%
Can get out and walk down road without difficulty *Table 6.1 (*65+)*	85	60	80	47
Can do household shopping on own *Table 6.1 (*65+)*	84	58	74	39
Has no difficulty with any domestic task *Table 4.6 (*65+)*	82	54	69	33
Has no difficulty with *any* task *Table 4.10 (*65+)*	71	44	61	25
Has no limiting long-standing illness *Table A.15*	59	51	64	46
Has gardened in last month *Table 3.1*	64	46	48	26
Has taken part in sporting activity in last month *Table 3.5*	57	21	40	12
Has given regular help to someone outside household *Fig 5.2 (*65+)*	39	17	35	9
In household in which holiday paid for in last three months *Table 3.8*	27	15	25	14
Has done voluntary work *Fig 5.6*	18	7	22	7
Has caring responsibilities *Fig 5.5a*	16	11	17	4
Does paid work *Table 2.1*	20	2	9	0

*lower cut-off point is 60 years unless otherwise stated.

Appendix A

The purpose of this appendix is to provide, with only the minimum of comment, Tables that may be of general interest, but have not been published elsewhere. We also provide updates of Tables that appeared in our previous report, which are of general interest, but are not directly relevant to the main report.

Population

Table A.1 Projected proportions of the elderly population in different age bands, from 1989-based projections and 1991-based projections, people aged 60 and over, United Kingdom, 1991–2021

	1991	1991	*2001*	2001	*2011*	2011	*2021*	2021
	%	%	%	%	%	%	%	%
60–64	*24.2*	24.2	*23.5*	23.3	*27.5*	27.2	*25.3*	24.7
65–69	*23.2*	23.3	*21.0*	20.9	*21.9*	21.6	*21.0*	20.7
70–74	*19.0*	19.1	*18.9*	19.0	*17.0*	17.0	*20.4*	20.3
75–79	*15.5*	15.6	*16.0*	16.0	*13.5*	13.6	*14.6*	14.6
80–84	*10.6*	10.4	*10.9*	10.8	*10.2*	10.2	*9.5*	9.6
85–89	*5.3*	5.4	*6.4*	6.4	*6.4*	6.4	*5.7*	5.9
90+	*2.2*	2.1	*3.3*	3.7	*3.5*	4.1	*3.4*	4.3

Source: 1991: Government Actuaries Department, final mid-1991 based projections, 1993 2001–2021: OPCS, 1995

(Update: Table 1.1, *Life After 60*, page 11)

Note: Figures in italics are 1989-based UK projections; others are 1991-based UK projections

Table A.1 is an update of **Table 1.1** in *Life After 60,* which was based on the 1989-based projections. This table compares the final mid–1991 population estimates and mid–1992 based projections with the old mid–1989 based principal projections of the Registrar General. Changes are evident from **Table A.1,** especially in the oldest age groups. In the next ten years, the very old (people aged 90 and over) are expected to make up 3.7% instead of 3.3% of the elderly population. By 2021, the 'old elderly' (people aged 80 and over) are expected to make up 20.4% of the elderly population, instead of only 18.6% of the elderly population.

Table A.2 Age structure of the population, by age group and gender, Great Britain, mid-1991

	males 000's	females 000's	total 000's
0–4	1,925	1,828	**3,753**
5–9	1,818	1,722	**3,540**
10–15	2,069	1,956	**4,026**
16–19	1,510	1,433	**2,942**
20–24	2,215	2,139	**4,354**
25–29	2,335	2,281	**4,616**
30–34	2,064	2,047	**4,111**
35–39	1,846	1,844	**3,690**
40–44	2,022	2,022	**4,044**
45–49	1,713	1,715	**3,428**
50–54	1,495	1,501	**2,996**
55–59	1,411	1,438	**2,849**
60–64	1,361	1,463	**2,824**
65–69	1,262	1,466	**2,728**
70–74	960	1,268	**2,228**
75–79	712	1,111	**1,823**
80–84	411	812	**1,223**
85–89	177	457	**634**
90+	49	198	**247**
Total	27,355	28,701	**56,056**

Source: Government Actuaries Department, final mid-1991 based projections, 1993.

Table A.3 Projected proportions of the population in broad age groups Great Britain, 1991–2041

	1991 %	2001 %	2011 %	2021 %	2031 %	2041 %
0–15	20.2	20.6	19.2	18.2	18.1	17.5
16–59	58.9	58.8	57.8	55.9	52.1	52.3
60–74	13.9	13.0	15.1	17.0	19.0	16.9
75+	7.0	7.6	7.9	8.9	10.8	13.3

Source: 1991: Government Actuaries Department, final mid-1991 based projections, 1993 2001–2041: OPCS, 1995

Twenty-one per cent of the population of Great Britain was currently aged 60 or over in 1991 (**Table A.3**). Substantial changes are expected to occur over the next 50 years, although, of course, any long term projection must be viewed with considerable caution. A slight decline in the proportion aged 60 and over will take place by the time of the next census, but thereafter the proportion will expand, mainly at the expense of the proportion in the working ages (15–59). In fifty years' time, we can expect 30% of the population to be aged 60 and over, and the proportion aged 75 and over will almost have doubled.

Table A.4 shows the changing age composition of the elderly population in finer detail. The 'young elderly' (60–69) are expected to form a smaller proportion of the elderly population (44.3% in 2031 compared with 47% in 1991). In contrast, the 'oldest old' (85 and over) will make up a steadily rising proportion of the elderly population, rising from 7.5% in 1991 to 10.2% in 2001 and 10.8% in 2031.

At most ages, the number of elderly people is expected to increase, even amongst the young elderly. We can expect to see a further 2.6 million people aged 60–69 by 2031. Amongst the oldest old (85 years and over) we can expect a further 1.1 million in forty years.

Table A.4 Projected changes in the age composition of the elderly population, by age group, people aged 60 and over, Great Britain, 1991–2041

	1991	2001	2011	2021	2031
	%	%	%	%	%
60–64 years	24.1	23.2	27.2	24.7	22.6
65–69 years	23.3	20.9	21.6	20.6	22.7
70–74 years	19.0	19.0	16.9	20.3	18.4
75–79 years	15.6	16.0	13.6	14.6	13.9
80–84 years	10.4	10.8	10.2	9.6	11.6
85–89 years	5.4	6.5	6.4	5.9	6.5
90 years & over	2.1	3.7	4.1	4.3	4.3
Population aged 60 yrs and over (000's)	11,707	11,950	13,691	15,594	18,023

Source: 1991: Government Actuaries Department, final mid-1991 based projections, 1993 2001–2031: OPCS, 1995

Table A.5 shows differences in marital status over the older age groups (note: these Figures are based on the resident population of Great Britain on Census night, 21 April 1991, and are therefore not exactly the same as the Figures in **Table A.2** which are based on the mid-1991 population projections). Although a slightly higher proportion of men were never-married in the youngest of the older age groups, considerably higher proportions of women at all ages over 75 were never-married. While 80% of men were married at ages 60–64, only just over two thirds of women were married; and while a fifth of men were still married at the age of 95 and over, only four per cent of women were. Half of all women were widowed by the age of 75; men did not reach this proportion until the age of 90.

Table A.5 Marital status, by age group and gender, resident population aged 60 and over of Great Britain, 1991

	Single	Married	Divorced	Widowed	N
	%	%	%	%	
Men					
60–64 years	8.6	80.7	5.6	5.1	1,359,362
65–69 years	8.1	78.6	4.1	9.2	1,264,364
70–74 years	7.1	75.8	3.1	14.0	950,060
75–79 years	6.7	69.2	2.3	21.8	709,876
80–84 years	6.6	59.4	1.6	32.4	407,166
85–89 years	6.7	46.6	1.2	45.5	160,253
90–94 years	6.4	31.7	0.9	60.9	37,386
95–99 years	6.6	20.5	1.1	71.8	5,514
100 years & over	16.2	20.6	1.4	61.8	1,055
Women					
60–64 years	6.5	68.5	6.2	18.8	1,464,395
65–69 years	7.2	58.6	4.7	29.6	1,473,043
70–74 years	7.8	46.3	3.5	42.3	1,257,827
75–79 years	9.2	32.4	2.5	55.9	1,109,505
80–84 years	11.2	20.1	1.7	66.9	808,711
85–89 years	13.2	11.1	1.2	74.5	437,585
90–94 years	13.9	5.7	0.7	79.7	151,213
95–99 years	15.4	3.5	0.5	80.6	31,568
100 years & over	16.2	4.3	0.8	78.8	6,104

Source: OPCS, 1993:p33

The general differences in marital status between men and women are clearly demonstrated in **Figure A.1**, which compares the marital status of all men aged 60 and over with that of all women aged 60 and over. Although almost the same proportions were divorced or single, three times the proportion of women were widowed. Three quarters of elderly men were still married, compared with less than half of the women.

Figure A.1 Marital status, by gender, people aged 60 and over, Great Britain, 1991

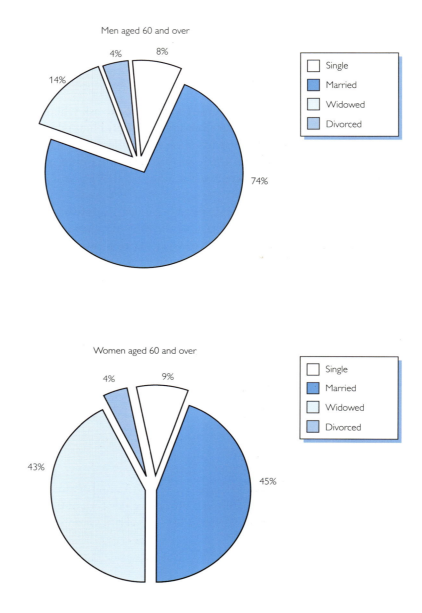

Source: OPCS 1991:p33

Table A.6, which updates **Table 2.3** in *Life After 60* from 1988 to 1991, shows the living arrangements of older people. There was little change since 1988, although slightly more men, especially at the older ages, lived alone in 1991, and slightly fewer lived with a spouse. There was very little change for women; the most obvious feature in 1991, as in 1988, was the big difference in the living arrangements of men and women.

Table A.6 Living arrangements, by age group and gender, people aged 60 and over, Great Britain, 1991

| | Men | | | | | | Women | | | | | |
	60–64 years	65–69 years	70–74 years	75–79 years	80 yrs & over	60 yrs & over	60–64 years	65–69 years	70–74 years	75–79 years	80 yrs & over	60 yrs & over
	%	%	%	%	%	%	%	%	%	%	%	%
Lives alone	12	16	20	28	38	**20**	23	33	43	56	64	**42**
With spouse	61	66	67	61	46	**61**	53	49	44	30	14	**40**
With spouse and others	24	13	9	6	5	**13**	14	7	4	3	1	**6**
With others (not spouse)	4	5	4	6	11	**5**	10	11	10	11	21	**12**
N (base)	578	557	417	338	273	**2,163**	641	698	524	480	512	**2,855**

Source: General Household Survey 1991

(Update: Table 2.3, *Life After 60,* page 20)

The 1991 Census was the first to ask whether people had a limiting long-term illness or not (defined as any health problem which limits daily activities). **Table A.7** shows that overall 37% of people living in households over pensionable age reported a long-term illness. At all ages over 75 significantly more women than men reported long-term illnesses.

Table A.7 Proportions with long-term limiting illness resident in households, by broad age group and gender, people over pensionable age, Great Britain, 1991

	Men		Women		Both	
	%	N	%	N	%	N
men 65–74, women 60–74	34.2	747,499	28.0	1,163,011	**30.1**	**1,910,510**
all 75–84 years	43.7	468,856	46.8	837,338	**45.6**	**1,306,194**
all 85 yrs & over	56.8	98,578	63.9	295,726	**62.0**	**394,304**
all 60 yrs & over	38.3	1,314,933	35.9	2,296,075	**36.7**	**3,611,008**

Source: 1991 Census, Local Base Statistics, Great Britain

Notes: standard census tables use 'pensionable age' rather than 60–74 or 65–74

Table A.8 shows the household composition of households containing residents of pensionable age. In 1991 7.3 million households contained one or more person of pensionable age. Forty-five per cent of these households comprised people living on their own, almost 80% of whom were women. Just over a quarter of households with one or more pensioners in them also contained non-pensioners. One third of all households in Great Britain contained pensioners.

Table A.8 Structure of households with one or more resident of pensionable age or over Great Britain, 1991

	N 000's	% of pensioner households	% of all households
Lone males	698.8	9.5	3.2
Lone females	2,603.5	35.5	11.9
Two or more pensioners	2,127.6	29.0	9.7
One or more pensioners with one or more non-pensioners	1,901.4	25.9	8.7
Total households with one or more pensioner(s)	7,331.3	100.0	33.5
Total number of households	21,897.0		100.0

Source: 1991 Census, Local Base Statistics, Great Britain. OPCS, July 1993

Table A.9 shows the proportion of pensioners living in households lacking certain amenities. In 1991, half of all pensioners lived in households without a car; but while only 40.5% of 'young elderly' people did not have access to a car in the household, 76.1% of the 'old elderly' did not have such access. The number of pensioners who did not have, or shared, a shower, bath or inside WC was 136,766 but again there are marked differences according to age. Four times the proportion of people aged 85 and over compared with people aged 60/65–74 lacked or shared such facilities. More than one in every five pensioners was without central heating.

Table A.9 Proportions of people of pensionable age and over living in households lacking certain amenities, Great Britain, 1991

	Lacking/sharing bath/shower and/or WC	No central heating	No car	Persons of pensionable age
	%	%	%	N
pensionable age to 74 years	0.9	20.9	40.5	6,329,604
75–84 years	2.0	25.7	64.5	2,856,509
85 years & over	3.4	28.3	76.1	634,017
all persons of pensionable age	1.4	22.8	49.8	9,820,130

Source: 1991 Census, Local Base Statistics, Great Britain, 1991

Table A.10 shows that in 1991 the ethnic composition of the elderly population was overwhelmingly white. Of all people aged 60 and over, 1.2% were black, or Indian, Pakistani or Bangladeshi.

Table A.10 Ethnic group, by gender, people aged 60 and over, Great Britain, 1991

	Men	Women	Men & women	%
	000's	000's	000's	
White	4,800.0	6,659.5	**11,459.5**	98.5
Black*	35.5	28.2	**63.7**	0.5
I/P/B†	44.7	35.6	**80.3**	0.7
Chinese	4.1	4.8	**8.9**	0.1
Asian	3.6	4.4	**8.0**	0.1
Other	7.1	7.5	**14.6**	0.1
Total	4,895.0	6,740.0	**11,635.0**	100.0

Source: 1991 Census, Local Base Statistics, Great Britain

Notes: * Black = black Caribbean, black African, black other

†I/P/B = Indian, Pakistani, Bangladeshi

Table A.11 gives rates by age and sex of the population of pensionable age resident in medical and care establishments. Overall, 15% of men aged 85 and over and 26% of women aged 85 and over were resident in a medical or care establishment in 1991. Proportions are much smaller for younger pensioners, with only one per cent of people of pensionable age to 74, and five per cent of people aged 75–84 resident in such establishments. Sixty-five per cent of men and 69% of women aged 85 and over resident in establishments were resident in private nursing or residential homes. Overall, 2.1% of male pensioners, and five per cent of female pensioners were living in medical or care establishments.

Table A.11 Population (non staff) resident in medical and care establishments, rates per 10,000 total population by gender and broad age group, Great Britain, 1991

	Men				Women			
	65–74 yrs*	75–84 yrs	85 yrs & over	N 000's	60–74 yrs*	75–84 yrs	85 yrs & over	N 000's
NHS hospitals/homes – psychiatric	13.5	23.5	39.6	6.4	9.5	26.9	56.3	12.7
NHS hospitals/homes – other	12.8	31.3	76.1	7.9	10.8	40.3	135.4	20.8
non-NHS hospitals – psychiatric	1.1	1.7	3.4	0.5	0.8	1.8	3.8	0.9
non-NHS hospitals – other	0.9	2.4	6.6	0.6	1.0	3.4	11.7	1.8
Local Authority Homes	24.1	93.5	361.8	23.2	19.9	139.4	566.1	70.5
Housing Association homes and hostels	4.9	10.2	31.8	2.9	2.7	16.4	58.6	8.0
Nursing homes (private)	27.1	117.5	449.2	28.3	27.8	202.0	777.5	99.1
Residential homes (private)	31.6	120.5	531.6	31.3	31.7	239.8	1003.0	122.1
Total	116.1	400.6	1500.0	101.1	104.2	670.0	2612.5	335.9

Source: 1991 Census, Local Base Statistics, Great Britain

*pensionable age to 74, i.e. men 65–74, women 60–74

Disability Table A.12 shows the proportions of disabled older people in each severity category in 1985, as defined by OPCS Disability Survey, by gender. For brief details see Appendix B, and for detailed information see Martin et al, 1988. Higher proportions of men aged 65 and over were in the lower severity categories (less disabled) compared with women. Just over a half of men were in severity categories one to four, compared with 41% of women. Thirty-seven per cent of men were severely disabled (categories five and above), compared with 48% of women.

Table A.12 Proportions of disabled people in different severity categories, by gender, disabled people aged 65 and over, Great Britain, 1985

Severity category	Men %	N weighted	N unweighted	Women %	N weighted	N unweighted
0	–	–	39	–	–	31
1	23	474	383	15	558	456
2	17	356	278	14	493	385
3	13	277	214	12	448	345
4	11	225	181	11	391	306
5	10	196	162	13	462	356
6	7	135	106	11	384	294
7	7	135	112	10	368	267
8	6	127	106	6	224	174
9	6	123	96	6	230	159
10	1	26	25	2	82	67

Source: Disability Survey 1985

Table A.13 Proportions of disabled adults in different severity categories, by age group and gender, people aged 65 and over, Great Britain, 1985

Severity category	65–69 years	70–74 years	75–79 years	80–84 years	85 yrs & over
	%	%	%	%	%
Men					
1	27	26	21	18	13
2	17	21	18	14	12
3	15	13	11	12	18
4	10	10	11	12	12
5	7	9	10	11	13
6	5	6	7	8	9
7	6	5	7	10	4
8	6	5	7	8	7
9	6	5	7	6	9
10	1	0	2	1	1
N (weighted)	537	571	489	313	163
N (unweighted)	460	493	390	246	113
Women					
1	20	20	14	15	7
2	18	16	15	11	7
3	11	15	14	13	6
4	12	11	13	10	7
5	15	10	13	12	13
6	7	11	11	11	13
7	8	7	10	12	16
8	3	6	5	6	11
9	5	4	4	6	15
10	1	1	1	4	5
N (weighted)	630	795	895	751	568
N (unweighted)	531	663	715	549	382

Source: Disability Survey 1985

At age 65–69, women tended to be slightly more disabled than men, although the differences were not large. Forty-four per cent of men were mildly impaired (categories one and two), compared with 38% of women. The same pattern is seen, though it is more pronounced, in older age groups. At age 75–79, 39% of disabled men are mildly impaired, compared with only 29% of disabled women. Forty per cent of men, and 44% of women were severely impaired (categories five and above). The most dramatic differences occur at the very oldest age, where 25% of men, but only 14% of women were mildly impaired, and 43% of men and 73% of women were severely impaired.

The overall picture for men is a steep decline in severity category one with age, balanced by a rise in the 'middle' severity categories four to six. The proportions in the more severe categories remained roughly the same with age, and with only very small proportions in category ten. The overall picture for women is rather different. There is, as with men, a steep decline in the proportions in category one with age, but this is balanced by a corresponding rise not in the 'middle' categories, but in the severe categories six to ten. A third of women aged 85 and over were very severely impaired (categories eight, nine and ten).

General health   Tables **A.14** and **A.15** update **Tables 6.1** and **6.4** in *Life after 60,* from 1988 to 1991. Many caveats have been noted concerning self-reported health status (Askham et al, 1992:p60; Bridgwood and Savage, 1993:p150), and these should always be borne in mind, especially when reflecting on trends over time. In fact, there was very little difference in self-reported health between 1988 and 1991, although in 1991 slightly larger proportions of men and women in all age groups reported their health as being 'good', generally at the expense of those reporting it as 'fairly good'. As in 1988, there was very little difference in the proportions of men reporting 'good' health at ages 75–79 and 80 and over. For women, however, there was a large and consistent drop over the age groups in the proportions reporting 'good' health, from half at age 60–64, to under a third at age 80 and over.

Table A.14 Self reported health, by age group and gender, people aged 60 and over, Great Britain, 1991

	60–64 years	65–69 years	70–74 years	75–79 years	80 yrs & over	60 yrs & over
	%	%	%	%	%	%
Men						
good	48	46	45	38	35	**44**
fairly good	30	35	37	36	38	**35**
not good	23	19	17	26	27	**22**
N (base)	551	538	406	326	260	**2,081**
Women						
good	50	45	39	37	30	**41**
fairly good	31	38	41	35	42	**37**
not good	19	16	21	29	27	**22**
N (base)	630	676	515	462	473	**2,756**

Source: General Household Survey, 1991

(Update: Table 6.1, *Life After 60*, page 60)

Table A.15 Limiting and non-limiting long-standing illness, by age group and gender, people aged 60 and over, Great Britain, 1991

	60–64 years	65–69 years	70–74 years	75–79 years	80 yrs & over	60 yrs & over
	%	%	%	%	%	%
Men						
Limiting long-standing illness	40	38	42	45	49	**42**
Non-limiting long-standing illness	16	21	22	18	15	**19**
No long-standing illness	44	41	36	38	36	**40**
N (base)	570	553	414	336	270	**2,143**
Women						
Limiting long-standing illness	29	32	38	48	54	**39**
Non-limiting long-standing illness	21	23	18	14	14	**18**
No long-standing illness	50	46	44	38	32	**43**
N (base)	637	691	521	476	507	**2,832**

Source: General Household Survey, 1991

(Update: Table 6.4, *Life After 60*, page 62)

Almost exactly the same proportions of men reported a limiting long-standing illness in 1991 as in 1988, but the proportions of women reporting one were considerably lower. In 1988, 44% of women overall reported a limiting long-standing illness, but in 1991, the proportion dropped to 39%. This was not balanced by a larger proportion reporting a non-limiting long-standing illness – this remained almost stationary, at roughly one woman in five – but in the proportion reporting no long-standing illness at all.

However, we see the same pattern as in 1988, with similar proportions of men over all age groups reporting limiting long-standing illnesses, but with steeply rising proportions of women reporting such illnesses – under a third at age 60-64, to over a half at age 80 and over.

It is interesting that while considerably lower proportions of women than men aged 60-74 reported a limiting long-standing illness, older women of all ages found it more difficult to undertake household and personal care tasks than men (see Chapter Four).

Housing

Table A.16 Housing tenure, by age group, people aged 60 and over and 16–59, Great Britain, 1991

	60–64 years	65–69 years	70–74 years	75–79 years	80 yrs & over	60 yrs & over	16–59 years
	%	%	%	%	%	%	%
Owned outright	51	55	53	51	51	**52**	14
Owned, with mortgage	21	10	7	5	6	**11**	59
All owned	**72**	**65**	**60**	**56**	**57**	**63**	**73**
Rented: Local Authority	21	29	30	30	32	**28**	18
Rented: Housing Association	2	3	4	6	5	**3**	2
Rented: Other	5	3	6	8	6	**6**	7
All rented	**28**	**35**	**40**	**44**	**43**	**37**	**27**
N (base)	1,215	1,252	939	815	784	**5,005**	**14,186**

Source: General Household Survey 1991

(Update: Table 3.1a, *Life After 60*, page 24)

There was a shift upwards between 1988 and 1991 in the proportions of people aged 60 and over living in owner-occupied homes, from 57% to 63%, with a corresponding decline in the proportions in rented property, from 43% to 37%. There were rises in the proportions in owner-occupied homes at all ages, but especially at age 60-64. Overall, in 1991 half of all people aged 60 and over lived in homes which were owned outright.

Figure A.2 Proportions of people living in owner-occupied property, by broad age group, people aged 60 and over and 16–59, Great Britain, 1979, 1988, 1991

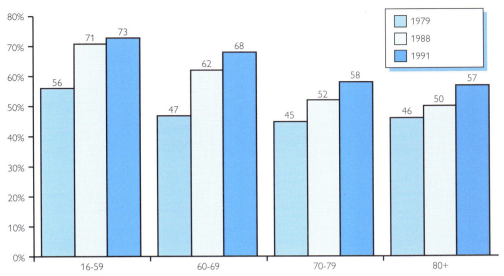

Source: Life After 60, Table 3.5; General Household Survey 1991

The substantial changes in owner occupation, clearly evident between 1979 and 1988 (*Life After 60,* **Table 3.5**, p 28), continued to 1991, with the largest proportional changes at the very oldest ages. In 1979 only 46% of people aged 80 and over lived in owner-occupied housing, and the proportion rose to only 50% in 1988. Only three years later, however, 57% of people aged 80 and over lived in homes which were owner-occupied.

Appendix B

The purpose of this appendix is to provide an easy reference guide to all the surveys and sources used in this report. It contains general information on each survey: which body carried it out, its purpose, coverage, and major publications associated with the survey. It also includes specific information, where relevant, on the particular annual survey used in the report, and on the status of GDS access to the source. Where it is indicated that the GDS has access to computerised data, interested parties may, if desired, request further tables from us, subject to the terms laid down by the depositor of the data and The Data Archive.

The sources/surveys are listed in alphabetical order, and comprise:

British Social Attitudes Survey	National Travel Survey
Census, 1991	OPCS Surveys of Disability
Family Expenditure Survey	Population estimates
General Household Survey	Population projections
International Passenger Survey	Survey of Retirement and Retirement Plans

British Social Attitudes Survey (BSAS)

Carried out by: Social and Community Planning Research.

Purpose: Measurement of long-run changes in values. Core questions are asked every year, generally on attitudes that are likely to change rapidly, along with different modules, e.g. on diet, health, divorce, in particular years. All modules are scheduled for repetition.

Coverage: Around 3,000 individuals in private households in Great Britain.

Publications: Yearly report by SCPR containing chapters on areas of particular interest for that year, appendices with details of sample design, weighting, sampling errors, analysis variables, and a full transcript of questionnaires. Also cumulative source book covering the first six surveys (SCPR, 1992).

GDS access to computerised data: Data tapes of all surveys from 1983 onwards, made available through The Data Archive.

Surveys used in this report: *BSAS 1986*
Social networks and support systems module. For the following relatives – mother, father, sister, brother, daughter, son – people were asked: is relative alive; if relative is alive, how often do you see or visit; how long does it take to get to relative; how often do you have any contact with relative, besides visiting, either by telephone or letter. Respondents were also asked how many grandparents, adult grandchildren, aunts and uncles, brothers/sisters in law and other relatives they had, which one they had most contact with, and type of contact. They were also asked how many close friends (not family members) they had, and type of contact with best friend, and several questions about social support (see Jarvis, 1993 for further details). 319 people were aged 60 and over, of whom 57% were women, 43% men (Jarvis, 1993). *BSAS 1991* for age at retirement.

Census, 1991

Carried out by: Office of Population Censuses and Surveys.

Coverage: Intended coverage 100%, actual coverage 98% (OPCS, 1993:p7). Certain groups of people are known to be under-enumerated; for example, men aged 20–29, men aged 85 and over. See OPCS, 1993:7.

Publications: (i) Procedures. Enumeration procedures, definitions, and a reproduction of the census form are published in the OPCS Topic Report, *1991 Census: definitions.* Summary information, and details of under enumeration and adjustment factors are given in the Topic Report *1991 Census: sex, age and marital status.* Detailed information on adjustments for under enumeration may be found in the OPCS Monitor series PP1.

(ii) Results. Results for Great Britain are initially published in the OPCS Topic Monitors, series CEN91. These are eventually published as full Topic Reports. The Monitors contain summary analyses of the final 1991 census figures, while the Topic Reports contain detailed analyses. A timetable giving dates for publication of the 1991 census analyses is available from the OPCS Information Branch.

GDS access to computerised data: Local base and small area statistics (gives access to a wide range of pre-defined tables). Sample of Anonymised Records – two per cent file for individuals, one per cent file for households (allows access to individual anonymised records, allowing creation of user-defined tables). Special terms of access apply.

Family Expenditure Survey

Carried out by: Office of Population Censuses and Surveys, on behalf of the Central Statistical Office (CSO) in Great Britain, and Policy Planning and Research Unit of Department of Finance and Personnel in Northern Ireland.

Purpose: A continuous survey of private households in the UK to provide information on household expenditure and income and other aspects of household finances. Used to prepare the Retail Prices Index. Also used by other government departments, such as housing and transport, as a basis for policy making.

Coverage: Sample of the general population resident in private non-institutional households. Around 7,000 households in the UK complete both the diary and the questionnaire parts of the survey each year. In 1991, the UK sample size was 7,056 households (CSO, 1992).

Publications: Reports are published every year by CSO.

GDS access to computerised data: Data tapes of all surveys from 1979 onwards made available through The Data Archive.

Surveys used in this report: 1991.

General Household Survey (GHS)

Carried out by: Office of Population Censuses and Surveys.

Purpose: Continuous multi-purpose survey of private households in Great Britain sponsored by several government departments. Its aim is to provide information on aspects of housing, employment, education, health and social services, transport, population and social security.

Coverage: Sample of the general population resident in private, non-institutional households. For 1991, for example, 19,039 people aged 16 and over living in 9,955 private households in Great Britain (Bridgwood and Savage, 1993:p1). The middle response rate for 1991 was 84%. **Table B.1** shows the sex and age structure of the elderly population from GHS 1991.

Table B.1 Proportions of men and women in the 1991 General Household Survey, by age group, people aged 60 and over

	Men	Women	N
	%	%	
60–64	47	53	1,219
65–69	44	56	1,255
70–74	44	56	941
75–79	41	59	818
80+	35	65	785
Total 60 and over	43	57	5,018

Source: General Household Survey, 1991

Appendix C of Bridgwood and Savage, 1993 compares the structure of the population sampled in the GHS with the 1991 census results, and discusses possible causes of the differences. For the purposes of this report, it should be noted that the age structure of males over the age of 60 is very close to that of the census, but women over 80 are under-represented in the GHS (5.1% of the total population in the census, compared with 4.1% of the population in the GHS; Bridgwood and Savage, 1993:p268).

Publications: Reports are published every year by OPCS in the series GHS.

GDS access to computerised data: Data tapes of all surveys from 1979 onwards made available through The Data Archive.

Surveys used in this report: *GHS 1987*
Special section on voluntary work undertaken in last 12 months, and on sports and physical exercises (new methodology). New sections on share ownership and attendance at various kinds of arts performances and museums, art galleries and public libraries (OPCS, 1989).

GHS 1990
New sections on tenants' attitudes to landlords, and people's reasons for drawing occupational pensions earlier or later than usual. Repeated questions on smoking, drinking and participation in sports activities. Special section on carers, similar to the one in GHS 1985 (Smyth and Browne, 1992).

Sporting and leisure activities
Participants were asked several questions about physical and leisure activities that they may have taken part in. The most general questions were whether or not they had been for a walk or a hike of two miles or more in the last twelve months, and whether or not they had undertaken one or more sporting activity in the last twelve months. This included training, coaching and refereeing. The list of sports ranged from swimming, soccer and bowls, to fishing, hunting and motor sports. Less vigorous sports were also included: keep-fit, snooker and darts.

GHS 1991

New questions about stepchildren, purchase of Local Authority housing, divorce, remarriage, housing tenure, personal pensions, sight tests. Also section on elderly people, similar to the one in GHS 1985 (Bridgwood and Savage, 1993:p1).

International Passenger Survey

Carried out by:	Office of Population Censuses and Surveys for the Department of National Heritage and a number of other government departments.
Purpose:	to collect data on travel expenditure, to provide detailed information on overseas visitors to the UK for tourism policy, to furnish data on international migration, and to provide travel information on routes used by passengers as an aid to aviation and shipping authorities.
Coverage:	In 1990, 165,000 interviews with travellers passing through passport control of all main air and sea ports of entrance to and exit from the UK (around 0.2% of all travellers). The sample is a multi-stage stratified random sample.
Publications:	Monthly estimates of volume of international visits and expenditure are published in the *CSO Bulletin and Employment Gazette*. Migration data is published in OPCS Monitors, series HN.
GDS access to computerised data:	None. Data tapes and tabulations may be obtained from the Department of National Heritage.
Surveys used in this report:	*1991* Tabulations were purchased from the Department of National Heritage, Statistics Division.

National Travel Survey, 1989/91

Carried out by:	Office of Population Censuses and Surveys (for the Department of Transport).
Purpose:	Continuous, small-scale survey of individuals in private households to provide personal information and details of travel made for private purposes or for work or education over a period of seven consecutive days. Details include journey purpose, method of travel, time of day, length of journey (GSS, 1993:p1). Demographic information is collected on a household questionnaire, the rest of the information on an individual questionnaire. Used to develop transport policies.
Coverage:	26,285 individuals in 10,752 private households in Great Britain, between January 1989 and December 1991. Response rate 79.8%. Women aged 75 and over are under-represented in the survey by an estimated 6%. Five surveys were carried out over 12 month periods between 1965 and 1985/6; more recent surveys are collected over a period of three years (data collection for the 1989/91 survey started in July 1988). Like the General Household Survey, the NTS has a complex design which clusters the sample before selection.
Publications:	Reports are published by the Government Statistical Service. See GSS, 1993, which also gives details of the five earlier surveys.
GDS access to computerised data:	No access at present.
Surveys used in this report:	*1989/91* Tabulations were purchased from the Department of Transport, Statistics Division.

OPCS Surveys of Disability in Great Britain, 1985–1988

Carried out by: Office of Population Censuses and Surveys.

Purpose: To provide information on the number of disabled people in Great Britain with different levels of severity and their circumstances for the purposes of planning benefits and services.

Coverage: Four surveys, carried out between 1985 and 1988, covering adults in private households, children in private households, adults in communal establishments, and children in communal establishments in Great Britain. The sample size for the survey of disabled adults in private households was 10,000 people. See Martin et al, (1988) for details of survey method and definitions of disability and measurement of severity.

Publications: Four reports by OPCS, published by HMSO in the series *OPCS surveys of disability in Great Britain,* 1988 and 1989.

GDS access to computerised data: Data tapes of surveys concerning disabled adults in private households (1985), and in communal establishments (1986), made available through The Data Archive.

Surveys used in this report: Survey of disabled adults in private households, 1985. Comprised two main parts: part one asked questions about the nature of the disabilities experienced by the interviewee, the answers being used to assess the type and severity of disability. Part two covered the circumstances of the disabled person, and examined the consequences of disability. Scales were developed in ten main areas of disability (see Martin, 1988:p10), and a formula was applied to everyone on the survey in order to calculate an overall severity score (Martin, 1988:p12). An example of severity category one is deaf in one ear; of severity category five, daily incontinence, cannot walk more then 50 yards without stopping; and of severity category ten, senility – cannot be understood by people who know person well, cannot feed self without help, daily incontinence, behavioural problems. For detailed 'pen pictures' of severity categories, (see Martin, 1988:p13–15).

Population Estimates

Carried out by: Population Estimates Unit at OPCS.

Publications: OPCS Monitor series PP1 contains information by sex and single-year age groups for England and Wales, and other key results. Occasional papers describe the methods used to derive the estimates (see, for example, *OPCS Occasional Paper 37),* and the journal of OPCS, *Population Trends,* often contains useful articles (see, for example, *Population Trends 73).*

GDS access to computerised data: Mid-1993 estimates for: England and Wales, by sex and single-year age groups; standard regions, counties and LA districts, by sex and five-year age groups; regional and district health authorities, by sex and five-year age bands. All made available through OPCS Population Estimates Unit.

Population Projections

Carried out by: Government Actuary's Department in consultation with the Registrars General. Final 1991-based projections are available, replacing the 1989-based projections. 1992-based projections now replace the previous set of 1991-based projections. In the medium term (to 2011) there is no projected difference at all in the proportions of the population of pensionable age (OPCS, 1994:p5), although in the longer term there are small differences. By 2011, for example, a projected 6.21% of men will be over 75, along with 9.59% of women (1992-based projection), compared with 6.62% and 9.75% respectively for the 1991-based projection. Changes were much larger between the 1991-based and 1989-based projections, with significant changes being made to all the underlying component assumptions (for example, lower long-term completed family size for the post-1965 birth cohorts, and greater improvements in mortality in the later projection). Diskettes containing the data are available for academic use from the Government Actuary's Department. Sub-national projections are prepared by the Population Projections unit at OPCS. At the time of writing, the mid-1992 sub-national projections (local government areas and Health Authorities) were not available.

Publications: OPCS Monitor series PP2 contains the key results, along with a broad indication of the assumptions concerning fertility, mortality and migration.

GDS access to computerised data: Latest projections for the UK and GB, made available by the Government Actuary's Department.

Survey of Retirement and Retirement Plans, 1988

Carried out by: Office of Population Censuses and Surveys, on behalf of Department of Social Security.

Purpose: Aid to planning policy on pensions and provisions for future pensioners. Main purposes: identify factors which influence the age at which people retire; help in the prediction of distribution of income after retirement; provide information about the financial preparations people make for retirement.

Coverage: 3,543 people aged 55–69 in private households in Great Britain in 1988.

Publications: Report published in 1992 (Bone et al, 1992).

GDS access to computerised data: Data tapes of full survey, made available through OPCS.

Appendix C

A note on sampling error and the statistics presented in this volume

All surveys, even large-scale surveys designed to be representative of the whole population, are subject to survey and sampling errors, and statistics derived from surveys are only useful if sampling errors are small for the purpose to which the statistics are put. If sampling errors are not small, conclusions drawn from survey statistics may be at best inappropriate, and at worst highly misleading. For this reason, it is good practice to estimate sampling error when considering the implications of statistical analyses.

Errors may occur because of:

1) the design and conduct of the survey, and non-response bias. This type of error may be reduced by re-weighting sample data. This type of survey error does not concern us here; all of the published reports on the large-scale surveys which we have used contain information on sample design and weighting where appropriate.

2) errors which are inherent in the sampling process. Sample means are estimates of the population mean, and will differ due to chance. The deviation of the sample mean from the population mean represents the estimation error, and is commonly called the standard error:

$$\text{standard error} = \sigma/\sqrt{n}$$

where σ = the standard deviation of the underlying population, and **n** = the sample size. The standard error therefore varies directly with the variability of the underlying population, and inversely with the square root of the sample size. It is clear that the standard error shrinks as sample size increases. In practice, of course, the standard deviation of the population is unknown, and is estimated using the standard deviation of the sample. Standard errors may be expressed in terms of confidence intervals about a sample mean. We have noted that the sample mean will differ from the true population mean due to chance; if we want to be confident that our inference is correct, we cannot claim that our sample mean is precisely equal to the population mean. We must construct a confidence interval of the form:

$$\mu = \bar{x} \pm \text{standard error}$$

where μ = population mean and $\bar{x}$ = sample mean. We must also decide how confident we wish to be that the sample estimate is correct. The most usual choices are the 95% confidence interval (95% chance that the sample mean will fall within plus or minus 1.96 standard errors of the population mean) or the 99% confidence interval (99% chance that the sample mean will fall within plus or minus 2.6 standard errors of the population mean). It should be noted that the above formula assumes that the sample is representative of the population, and is obtained by single-stage random selection. Simple random samples, however, are prohibitively expensive and all household surveys use a complex design which stratifies and clusters the sample before selection. More elaborate formulae may be used to take the main features of survey design into account; (see, for example, Breeze, 1990), which reports on design factors which show how standard errors are changed by the clustering and stratification of the sample; (CSO, 1994; GSS, 1993; and Butcher and Elliot, 1987). Design factors tend to lead to larger standard errors. It should also be noted that in this report individuals rather than households or families have been used as the unit of analysis. An advantage of the individual as a unit of analysis is that it avoids ambiguities over terms such as 'elderly households', which might be defined variously as: households headed by someone over a particular age; households containing *only* members over a particular age; and so on. However, one factor to bear in mind is that the *sampling* unit for the FES and GHS is the household. The samples of individuals they yield therefore contain clusters of individuals within households. In some circumstances (e.g. in data on incomes) households or families may be more appropriate units of analysis than individuals.

We noted earlier that when sample sizes are small, the standard error may be so large that means or proportions should only be regarded as rough indicators. Consider Figure C.1 which shows the 99% confidence intervals associated with Table 4.17, the proportions of people aged 60 and over possessing microwave ovens.

Figure C.1 99% confidence intervals: proportions possessing microwaves, by age group, people aged 60 and over, Great Britain

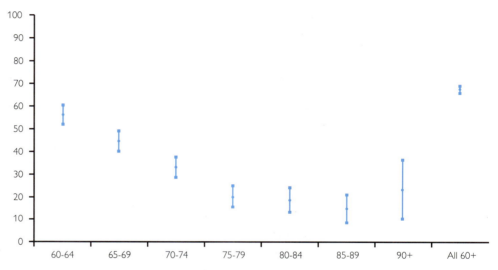

Source: General Household Survey 1991

Where the sample sizes are large, as with all people aged 60 and over (sample size 5,010), the confidence intervals around the sample proportion are small: the sample proportion is 68%, and we can be 99% sure that the proportion really lies between 66% and 70%. Where sample sizes are over 1,000 (people aged 60–64 and people aged 65–69) the confidence intervals are also acceptably small: for people aged 60–64, the sample proportion is 57%, and the 99% confidence interval is 53% to 61%. For people aged 65–69, the sample proportion is 45%, and the 99% confidence interval is 41% to 49%. As the sample sizes decrease, the confidence intervals become larger until, for ages 90 and above, the sample proportion is 22%, but we can be 99% confident only that the true proportion lies between 10% and 34%. (The true confidence intervals will be larger – the method assumes simple random sampling.)

Because of the interest in people aged 90 and over, we have on occasion presented proportions for this age group; it is clear that they must only be regarded as very rough estimates.

References

Allied Dunbar (1992) *Allied Dunbar National Fitness Survey: summary of the major findings and messages* Health Education Authority, London

Askham J, Barry C, Grundy E, Hancock R and Tinker A (1992) *Life after 60. A profile of Britain's older population* ACIOG, London

Bone M, Gregory J, Gill B and Loder D (1992) *Retirement and retirement plans. A survey carried out by Social Survey Division of OPCS on behalf of the Department of Social Security* HMSO, London

Breeze, E (1990) *General Household Survey. Report on sampling error: based on 1985 and 1986 data* HMSO, London

Bridgwood A and Savage D (1993) *General Household Survey 1991. An interdepartmental survey carried out by OPCS between April 1991 and March 1993* HMSO, London

Butcher B and Elliot D (1987) *A sampling errors manual* HMSO, London

Central Statistical Office (1992) *Family spending: a report on the 1991 Family Expenditure Survey* HMSO, London

Central Statistical Office (1994) *Family spending: a report on the 1993 Family Expenditure Survey* HMSO, London

Felstead A and Jewson N (1995) Working at home: estimates from the 1991 Census, Employment Gazette, March, 95–99

Goddard E and Savage D (1994) *People aged 65 and over. A study carried out on behalf of the Department of Health as part of the 1991 General Household Survey* Series GHS no. 22 Supplement A, HMSO, London

Government Actuary (1994) *Occupational pension schemes 1991* HMSO, London

Government Actuary's Department (1993) *Population projections, 1991–2061. Population projection by sex and age for Great Britain prepared by the Government Actuary in consultation with the Registrars General*

Government Statistical Service (1993) *Transport statistics report, National Travel Survey, 1989/91* HMSO: London

Hancock, R and Weir, P (1994) *More ways than means: a guide to pensioners' incomes in Great Britain in the 1980s,* ACIOG, London

Jarvis C (1993) *Family and friends in old age, and the implications for informal support* Joseph Rowntree Foundation Working Paper 6, ACIOG, London

Martin J, Meltzer H and Elliot D (1988) *OPCS surveys of disability in Great Britain. Report 1. The prevalence of disability among adults* HMSO, London

Matheson J (1991) *General Household Survey 1987 Participation in sport. A study carried out on behalf of the Department of the Environment as part of the 1987 General Household Survey* Series GHS no 17 Supplement B, HMSO, London

Office of Population Censuses and Surveys (1989) *General Household Survey 1987. An inter-departmental survey sponsored by the Central Statistical Office* HMSO, London

Office of Population Censuses and Surveys (1992) *1991 Census. Definitions. Great Britain* HMSO, London

Office of Population Censuses and Surveys (1992a) *General Household Survey: carers in 1990* OPCS Monitor SS92/2, London

Office of Population Censuses and Surveys (1993) *1991 Census. Sex, age and marital status. Great Britain* HMSO, London

Office of Population Censuses and Surveys (June 1993) *1991 Census. Topic monitor: limiting long-term illness. Great Britain* GSS, London

Office of Population Censuses and Surveys (July 1993) *1991 Census. Topic monitor: persons aged 60 and over. Great Britain* GSS, London

Office of Population Censuses and Surveys (1994) *National projections: 1992-based* OPCS Monitor PP2 94/1, GSS, London

Office of Population Censuses and Surveys (1995) *National population projections: 1992-based* OPCS Monitor PP2 no. 19, HMSO, London

Pahl, J (1990) Household spending, personal spending and the control of money in marriage **Sociology,** 24, 1, 119–138

Secretary of State for Health (1992) *The Health of the Nation: A Strategy for Health in England,* HMSO, London

Social and Community Planning Research (1992) *British Social Attitudes Cumulative Sourcebook: the first six surveys* Gower, Aldershot

Smyth M and Browne F (1992) *General Household Survey 1990. An inter-departmental survey carried out by OPCS between April 1990 amd March 1991* HMSO, London

Printed in the United Kingdom for HMSO
Dd 0301748   C15   5/96   3400/4   65536   350136   14/35012